Big Data Fundamentals

Big Data Fundamentals

Concepts, Drivers & Techniques

Thomas Erl,
Wajid Khattak,
and Paul Buhler

PRENTICE HALL

PRENTICE HALL
BOSTON • COLUMBUS • INDIANAPOLIS • NEW YORK • SAN FRANCISCO
AMSTERDAM • CAPE TOWN • DUBAI • LONDON • MADRID • MILAN • MUNICH
PARIS • MONTREAL • TORONTO • DELHI • MEXICO CITY • SAO PAULO
SIDNEY • HONG KONG • SEOUL • SINGAPORE • TAIPEI • TOKYO

For information about buying this title in bulk quantities, or for special sales opportunities (which may include electronic versions; custom cover designs; and content particular to your business, training goals, marketing focus, or branding interests), please contact our corporate sales department at corpsales@pearsoned.com or (800) 382-3419.

For government sales inquiries, please contact governmentsales@pearsoned.com.

For questions about sales outside the U.S., please contact international@pearsoned.com.

Visit us on the Web: informit.com/ph

Library of Congress Control Number: 2015953680

ISBN-13: 978-0-13-429107-9
ISBN-10: 0-13-429107-7

Text printed in the United States on recycled paper at RR Donnelley in Crawfordsville, Indiana.

First printing: December 2015

Editor-in-Chief
Mark Taub

Senior Acquisitions Editor
Trina MacDonald

Managing Editor
Kristy Hart

Senior Project Editor
Betsy Gratner

Copyeditors
Natalie Gitt
Alexandra Kropova

Senior Indexer
Cheryl Lenser

Proofreaders
Alexandra Kropova
Debbie Williams

Publishing Coordinator
Olivia Basegio

Cover Designer
Thomas Erl

Compositor
Bumpy Design

Graphics
Jasper Paladino

Photos
Thomas Erl

Educational Content Development
Arcitura Education Inc.

To my family and friends.
—Thomas Erl

I dedicate this book to my daughters Hadia and Areesha,
my wife Natasha, and my parents.

—Wajid Khattak

I thank my wife and family for their patience and for
putting up with my busyness over the years.

I appreciate all the students and colleagues I have had the
privilege of teaching and learning from.
John 3:16, 2 Peter 1:5-8

—Paul Buhler, PhD

Contents at a Glance

Contents

Chapter 2: Business Motivations and Drivers for Big Data Adoption. 29

Chapter 3: Big Data Adoption and Planning Considerations 47

PART II: STORING AND ANALYZING BIG DATA

CHAPTER 5: Big Data Storage Concepts. 91

Acknowledgments

In alphabetical order by last name:

- Allen Afuah, Ross School of Business, University of Michigan

- Thomas Davenport, Babson College

- Hugh Dubberly, Dubberly Design Office

- Joe Gollner, Gnostyx Research Inc.

- Dominic Greenwood, Whitestein Technologies

- Gareth Morgan, The Schulich School of Business, York University

- Peter Morville, Semantic Studios

- Michael Porter, The Institute for Strategy and Competitiveness, Harvard Business School

- Mark von Rosing, LEADing Practice

- Jeanne Ross, Center for Information Systems Research, MIT Sloan School of Management

- Jim Sinur, Flueresque

- John Sterman, MIT System Dynamics Group, MIT Sloan School of Management

Special thanks to the Arcitura Education and Big Data Science School research and development teams that produced the Big Data Science Certified Professional (BDSCP) course modules upon which this book is based.

Reader Services

Register your copy of *Big Data Fundamentals* at informit.com for convenient access to downloads, updates, and corrections as they become available. To start the registration process, go to informit.com/register and log in or create an account.* Enter the product ISBN, 9780134291079, and click Submit. Once the process is complete, you will find any available bonus content under "Registered Products."

*Be sure to check the box that you would like to hear from us in order to receive exclusive discounts on future editions of this product.

Part I

The Fundamentals of Big Data

Big Data has the ability to change the nature of a business. In fact, there are many firms whose sole existence is based upon their capability to generate insights that only Big Data can deliver. This first set of chapters covers the essentials of Big Data, primarily from a business perspective. Businesses need to understand that Big Data is not just about technology—it is also about how these technologies can propel an organization forward.

Part I has the following structure:

- Chapter 1 delivers insight into key concepts and terminology that define the very essence of Big Data and the promise it holds to deliver sophisticated business insights. The various characteristics that distinguish Big Data datasets are explained, as are definitions of the different types of data that can be subject to its analysis techniques.

- Chapter 2 seeks to answer the question of why businesses should be motivated to adopt Big Data as a consequence of underlying shifts in the marketplace and business world. Big Data is not a technology related to business transformation; instead, it enables innovation within an enterprise on the condition that the enterprise acts upon its insights.

- Chapter 3 shows that Big Data is not simply "business as usual," and that the decision to adopt Big Data must take into account many business and technology considerations. This underscores the fact that Big Data opens an enterprise to external data influences that must be governed and managed. Likewise, the Big Data analytics lifecycle imposes distinct processing requirements.

- Chapter 4 examines current approaches to enterprise data warehousing and business intelligence. It then expands this notion to show that Big Data storage and analysis resources can be used in conjunction with corporate performance monitoring tools to broaden the analytic capabilities of the enterprise and deepen the insights delivered by Business Intelligence.

Big Data used correctly is part of a strategic initiative built upon the premise that the internal data within a business does not hold all the answers. In other words, Big Data is not simply about data management problems that can be solved with technology. It is about business problems whose solutions are enabled by technology that can support the analysis of Big Data datasets. For this reason, the business-focused discussion in Part I sets the stage for the technology-focused topics covered in Part II.

Chapter 1

Understanding Big Data

Concepts and Terminology

Big Data Characteristics

Different Types of Data

Case Study Background

Big Data is a field dedicated to the analysis, processing, and storage of large collections of data that frequently originate from disparate sources. Big Data solutions and practices are typically required when traditional data analysis, processing and storage technologies and techniques are insufficient. Specifically, Big Data addresses distinct requirements, such as the combining of multiple unrelated datasets, processing of large amounts of unstructured data and harvesting of hidden information in a time-sensitive manner.

Although Big Data may appear as a new discipline, it has been developing for years. The management and analysis of large datasets has been a long-standing problem—from labor-intensive approaches of early census efforts to the actuarial science behind the calculations of insurance premiums. Big Data science has evolved from these roots.

In addition to traditional analytic approaches based on statistics, Big Data adds newer techniques that leverage computational resources and approaches to execute analytic algorithms. This shift is important as datasets continue to become larger, more diverse, more complex and streaming-centric. While statistical approaches have been used to approximate measures of a population via sampling since Biblical times, advances in computational science have allowed the processing of entire datasets, making such sampling unnecessary.

The analysis of Big Data datasets is an interdisciplinary endeavor that blends mathematics, statistics, computer science and subject matter expertise. This mixture of skill-sets and perspectives has led to some confusion as to what comprises the field of Big Data and its analysis, for the response one receives will be dependent upon the perspective of whoever is answering the question. The boundaries of what constitutes a Big Data problem are also changing due to the ever-shifting and advancing landscape of software and hardware technology. This is due to the fact that the definition of Big Data takes into account the impact of the data's characteristics on the design of the solution environment itself. Thirty years ago, one gigabyte of data could amount to a Big Data problem and require special purpose computing resources. Now, gigabytes of data are commonplace and can be easily transmitted, processed and stored on consumer-oriented devices.

Data within Big Data environments generally accumulates from being amassed within the enterprise via applications, sensors and external sources. Data processed by a Big

Data solution can be used by enterprise applications directly or can be fed into a data warehouse to enrich existing data there. The results obtained through the processing of Big Data can lead to a wide range of insights and benefits, such as:

- operational optimization

- actionable intelligence

- identification of new markets

- accurate predictions

- fault and fraud detection

- more detailed records

- improved decision-making

- scientific discoveries

Evidently, the applications and potential benefits of Big Data are broad. However, there are numerous issues that need to be considered when adopting Big Data analytics approaches. These issues need to be understood and weighed against anticipated benefits so that informed decisions and plans can be produced. These topics are discussed separately in Part II.

Concepts and Terminology

As a starting point, several fundamental concepts and terms need to be defined and understood.

Datasets

Collections or groups of related data are generally referred to as datasets. Each group or dataset member (datum) shares the same set of attributes or properties as others in the same dataset. Some examples of datasets are:

- tweets stored in a flat file

- a collection of image files in a directory

- an extract of rows from a database table stored in a CSV formatted file

- historical weather observations that are stored as XML files

Figure 1.1 shows three datasets based on three different data formats.

Figure 1.1

Datasets can be found in many different formats.

datasets

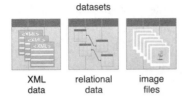

XML
data

relational
data

image
files

Data Analysis

Data analysis is the process of examining data to find facts, relationships, patterns, insights and/or trends. The overall goal of data analysis is to support better decision-making. A simple data analysis example is the analysis of ice cream sales data in order to determine how the number of ice cream cones sold is related to the daily temperature. The results of such an analysis would support decisions related to how much ice cream a store should order in relation to weather forecast information. Carrying out data analysis helps establish patterns and relationships among the data being analyzed. Figure 1.2 shows the symbol used to represent data analysis.

Figure 1.2

The symbol used to represent data analysis.

Data Analytics

Data analytics is a broader term that encompasses data analysis. Data analytics is a discipline that includes the management of the complete data lifecycle, which encompasses collecting, cleansing, organizing, storing, analyzing and governing data. The term includes the development of analysis methods, scientific techniques and automated tools. In Big Data environments, data analytics has developed methods that allow data analysis to occur through the use of highly scalable distributed technologies and frameworks that are capable of analyzing large volumes of data from different sources. Figure 1.3 shows the symbol used to represent analytics.

The Big Data analytics lifecycle generally involves identifying, procuring, preparing and analyzing large amounts of raw, unstructured data to extract meaningful information that can serve as an input for identifying patterns, enriching existing enterprise data and performing large-scale searches.

Different kinds of organizations use data analytics tools and techniques in different ways. Take, for example, these three sectors:

Figure 1.3
The symbol used to represent data analytics.

- In business-oriented environments, data analytics results can lower operational costs and facilitate strategic decision-making.

- In the scientific domain, data analytics can help identify the cause of a phenomenon to improve the accuracy of predictions.

- In service-based environments like public sector organizations, data analytics can help strengthen the focus on delivering high-quality services by driving down costs.

Data analytics enable data-driven decision-making with scientific backing so that decisions can be based on factual data and not simply on past experience or intuition alone. There are four general categories of analytics that are distinguished by the results they produce:

- descriptive analytics

- diagnostic analytics

- predictive analytics

- prescriptive analytics

The different analytics types leverage different techniques and analysis algorithms. This implies that there may be varying data, storage and processing requirements to facilitate the delivery of multiple types of analytic results. Figure 1.4 depicts the reality that the generation of high value analytic results increases the complexity and cost of the analytic environment.

Figure 1.4

Value and complexity increase from descriptive to prescriptive analytics.

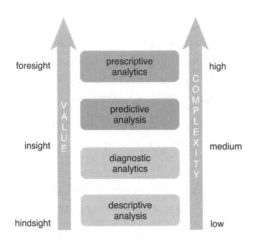

Descriptive Analytics

Descriptive analytics are carried out to answer questions about events that have already occurred. This form of analytics contextualizes data to generate information.

Sample questions can include:

- What was the sales volume over the past 12 months?
- What is the number of support calls received as categorized by severity and geographic location?
- What is the monthly commission earned by each sales agent?

It is estimated that 80% of generated analytics results are descriptive in nature. Value-wise, descriptive analytics provide the least worth and require a relatively basic skillset.

Descriptive analytics are often carried out via ad-hoc reporting or dashboards, as shown in Figure 1.5. The reports are generally static in nature and display historical data that is presented in the form of data grids or charts. Queries are executed on operational data stores from within an enterprise, for example a Customer Relationship Management system (CRM) or Enterprise Resource Planning (ERP) system.

Figure 1.5

The operational systems, pictured left, are queried via descriptive analytics tools to generate reports or dashboards, pictured right.

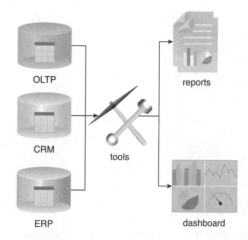

OLTP   tools   reports

CRM

ERP   dashboard

Diagnostic Analytics

Diagnostic analytics aim to determine the cause of a phenomenon that occurred in the past using questions that focus on the reason behind the event. The goal of this type of analytics is to determine what information is related to the phenomenon in order to enable answering questions that seek to determine why something has occurred.

Such questions include:

- Why were Q2 sales less than Q1 sales?

- Why have there been more support calls originating from the Eastern region than from the Western region?

- Why was there an increase in patient re-admission rates over the past three months?

Diagnostic analytics provide more value than descriptive analytics but require a more advanced skillset. Diagnostic analytics usually require collecting data from multiple sources and storing it in a structure that lends itself to performing drill-down and roll-up analysis, as shown in Figure 1.6. Diagnostic analytics results are viewed via interactive visualization tools that enable users to identify trends and patterns. The executed queries are more complex compared to those of descriptive analytics and are performed on multi-dimensional data held in analytic processing systems.

Figure 1.6

Diagnostic analytics can result in data that is suitable for performing drill-down and roll-up analysis.

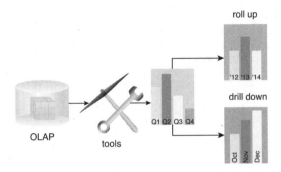

Predictive Analytics

Predictive analytics are carried out in an attempt to determine the outcome of an event that might occur in the future. With predictive analytics, information is enhanced with meaning to generate knowledge that conveys how that information is related. The strength and magnitude of the associations form the basis of models that are used to generate future predictions based upon past events. It is important to understand that the models used for predictive analytics have implicit dependencies on the conditions under which the past events occurred. If these underlying conditions change, then the models that make predictions need to be updated.

Questions are usually formulated using a what-if rationale, such as the following:

- What are the chances that a customer will default on a loan if they have missed a monthly payment?

- What will be the patient survival rate if Drug B is administered instead of Drug A?

- If a customer has purchased Products A and B, what are the chances that they will also purchase Product C?

Predictive analytics try to predict the outcomes of events, and predictions are made based on patterns, trends and exceptions found in historical and current data. This can lead to the identification of both risks and opportunities.

This kind of analytics involves the use of large datasets comprised of internal and external data and various data analysis techniques. It provides greater value and requires a more advanced skillset than both descriptive and diagnostic analytics. The tools used generally abstract underlying statistical intricacies by providing user-friendly front-end interfaces, as shown in Figure 1.7.

Figure 1.7

Predictive analytics tools can provide user-friendly front-end interfaces.

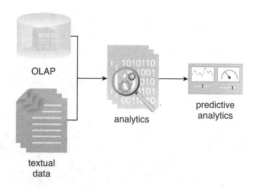

OLAP

textual data

analytics

predictive analytics

Prescriptive Analytics

Prescriptive analytics build upon the results of predictive analytics by prescribing actions that should be taken. The focus is not only on which prescribed option is best to follow, but why. In other words, prescriptive analytics provide results that can be reasoned about because they embed elements of situational understanding. Thus, this kind of analytics can be used to gain an advantage or mitigate a risk.

Sample questions may include:

• Among three drugs, which one provides the best results?

• When is the best time to trade a particular stock?

Prescriptive analytics provide more value than any other type of analytics and correspondingly require the most advanced skillset, as well as specialized software and tools. Various outcomes are calculated, and the best course of action for each outcome is suggested. The approach shifts from explanatory to advisory and can include the simulation of various scenarios.

This sort of analytics incorporates internal data with external data. Internal data might include current and historical sales data, customer information, product data and business rules. External data may include social media data, weather forecasts and government-produced demographic data. Prescriptive analytics involve the use of business rules and large amounts of internal and external data to simulate outcomes and prescribe the best course of action, as shown in Figure 1.8.

Figure 1.8

Prescriptive analytics involves the use of business rules and internal and/or external data to perform an in-depth analysis.

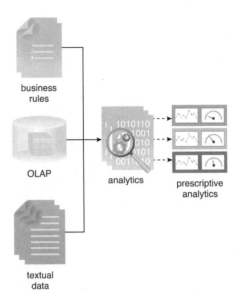

Business Intelligence (BI)

BI enables an organization to gain insight into the performance of an enterprise by analyzing data generated by its business processes and information systems. The results of the analysis can be used by management to steer the business in an effort to correct detected issues or otherwise enhance organizational performance. BI applies analytics to large amounts of data across the enterprise, which has typically been consolidated into an enterprise data warehouse to run analytical queries. As shown in Figure 1.9, the output of BI can be surfaced to a dashboard that allows managers to access and analyze the results and potentially refine the analytic queries to further explore the data.

Figure 1.9

BI can be used to improve business applications, consolidate data in data warehouses and analyze queries via a dashboard.

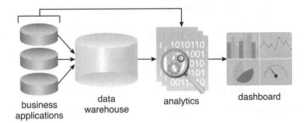

Key Performance Indicators (KPI)

A KPI is a metric that can be used to gauge success within a particular business context. KPIs are linked with an enterprise's overall strategic goals and objectives. They are often used to identify business performance problems and demonstrate regulatory compliance. KPIs therefore act as quantifiable reference points for measuring a specific aspect of a business' overall performance. KPIs are often displayed via a KPI dashboard, as shown in Figure 1.10. The dashboard consolidates the display of multiple KPIs and compares the actual measurements with threshold values that define the acceptable value range of the KPI.

Figure 1.10
A KPI dashboard acts as a central reference point for gauging business performance.

KPI dashboard

Big Data Characteristics

For a dataset to be considered Big Data, it must possess one or more characteristics that require accommodation in the solution design and architecture of the analytic environment. Most of these data characteristics were initially identified by Doug Laney in early 2001 when he published an article describing the impact of the volume, velocity and variety of e-commerce data on enterprise data warehouses. To this list, veracity has been added to account for the lower signal-to-noise ratio of unstructured data as compared to structured data sources. Ultimately, the goal is to conduct analysis of the data in such a manner that high-quality results are delivered in a timely manner, which provides optimal value to the enterprise.

This section explores the five Big Data characteristics that can be used to help differentiate data categorized as "Big" from other forms of data. The five Big Data traits shown in Figure 1.11 are commonly referred to as the Five Vs:

- volume

- velocity

- variety

- veracity

- value

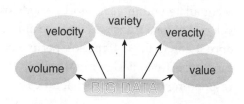

Figure 1.11
The Five Vs of Big Data.

Volume

The anticipated volume of data that is processed by Big Data solutions is substantial and ever-growing. High data volumes impose distinct data storage and processing demands, as well as additional data preparation, curation and management processes. Figure 1.12 provides a visual representation of the large volume of data being created daily by organizations and users world-wide.

Figure 1.12

Organizations and users world-wide create over 2.5 EBs of data a day. As a point of comparison, the Library of Congress currently holds more than 300 TBs of data.

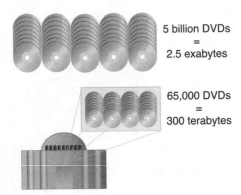

5 billion DVDs
=
2.5 exabytes

65,000 DVDs
=
300 terabytes

Typical data sources that are responsible for generating high data volumes can include:

- online transactions, such as point-of-sale and banking

- scientific and research experiments, such as the Large Hadron Collider and Atacama Large Millimeter/Submillimeter Array telescope

- sensors, such as GPS sensors, RFIDs, smart meters and telematics

- social media, such as Facebook and Twitter

Velocity

In Big Data environments, data can arrive at fast speeds, and enormous datasets can accumulate within very short periods of time. From an enterprise's point of view, the velocity of data translates into the amount of time it takes for the data to be processed once it enters the enterprise's perimeter. Coping with the fast inflow of data requires the enterprise to design highly elastic and available data processing solutions and corresponding data storage capabilities.

Depending on the data source, velocity may not always be high. For example, MRI scan images are not generated as frequently as log entries from a high-traffic webserver. As illustrated in Figure 1.13, data velocity is put into perspective when considering that the following data volume can easily be generated in a given minute: 350,000 tweets, 300 hours of video footage uploaded to YouTube, 171 million emails and 330 GBs of sensor data from a jet engine.

Figure 1.13

Examples of high-velocity Big Data datasets produced every minute include tweets, video, emails and GBs generated from a jet engine.

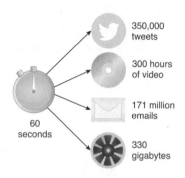

350,000 tweets

300 hours of video

171 million emails

330 gigabytes

60 seconds

Variety

Data variety refers to the multiple formats and types of data that need to be supported by Big Data solutions. Data variety brings challenges for enterprises in terms of data integration, transformation, processing, and storage. Figure 1.14 provides a visual representation of data variety, which includes structured data in the form of financial transactions, semi-structured data in the form of emails and unstructured data in the form of images.

structured data | texual data | image files | video | audio | XML data | JSON data | sensor data | metadata

Figure 1.14

Examples of high-variety Big Data datasets include structured, textual, image, video, audio, XML, JSON, sensor data and metadata.

Veracity

Veracity refers to the quality or fidelity of data. Data that enters Big Data environments needs to be assessed for quality, which can lead to data processing activities to resolve invalid data and remove noise. In relation to veracity, data can be part of the signal or noise of a dataset. Noise is data that cannot be converted into information and thus has no value, whereas signals have value and lead to meaningful information. Data with a high signal-to-noise ratio has more veracity than data with a lower ratio. Data that is acquired in a controlled manner, for example via online customer registrations, usually contains less noise than data acquired via uncontrolled sources, such as blog postings. Thus the signal-to-noise ratio of data is dependent upon the source of the data and its type.

Value

Value is defined as the usefulness of data for an enterprise. The value characteristic is intuitively related to the veracity characteristic in that the higher the data fidelity, the more value it holds for the business. Value is also dependent on how long data processing takes because analytics results have a shelf-life; for example, a 20 minute delayed stock quote has little to no value for making a trade compared to a quote that is 20 milliseconds old. As demonstrated, value and time are inversely related. The longer it takes for data to be turned into meaningful information, the less value it has for a business. Stale results inhibit the quality and speed of informed decision-making. Figure 1.15 provides two illustrations of how value is impacted by the veracity of data and the timeliness of generated analytic results.

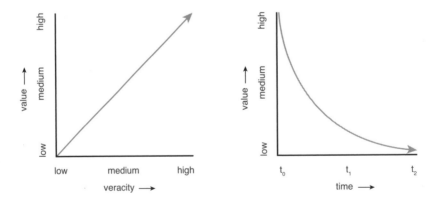

Figure 1.15
Data that has high veracity and can be analyzed quickly has more value to a business.

Apart from veracity and time, value is also impacted by the following lifecycle-related concerns:

- How well has the data been stored?

- Were valuable attributes of the data removed during data cleansing?

- Are the right types of questions being asked during data analysis?

- Are the results of the analysis being accurately communicated to the appropriate decision-makers?

Different Types of Data

The data processed by Big Data solutions can be human-generated or machine-generated, although it is ultimately the responsibility of machines to generate the analytic results. Human-generated data is the result of human interaction with systems, such as online services and digital devices. Figure 1.16 shows examples of human-generated data.

Figure 1.16

Examples of human-generated data include social media, blog posts, emails, photo sharing and messaging.

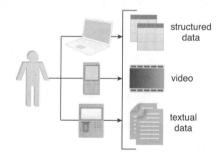

Machine-generated data is generated by software programs and hardware devices in response to real-world events. For example, a log file captures an authorization decision made by a security service, and a point-of-sale system generates a transaction against inventory to reflect items purchased by a customer. From a hardware perspective, an example of machine-generated data would be information conveyed from the numerous sensors in a cellphone that may be reporting information, including position and cell tower signal strength. Figure 1.17 provides a visual representation of different types of machine-generated data.

Figure 1.17

Examples of machine-generated
data include web logs, sensor
data, telemetry data, smart meter
data and appliance usage data.

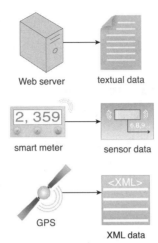

As demonstrated, human-generated and machine-generated data can come from a variety of sources and be represented in various formats or types. This section examines the variety of data types that are processed by Big Data solutions. The primary types of data are:

- structured data

- unstructured data

- semi-structured data

These data types refer to the internal organization of data and are sometimes called data formats. Apart from these three fundamental data types, another important type of data in Big Data environments is metadata. Each will be explored in turn.

Structured Data

Structured data conforms to a data model or schema and is often stored in tabular form. It is used to capture relationships between different entities and is therefore most often stored in a relational database. Structured data is frequently generated by enterprise applications and information systems like ERP and CRM systems. Due to the abundance of tools and databases that natively support structured data, it rarely requires

Figure 1.18

The symbol used to represent structured data stored in a tabular form.

special consideration in regards to processing or storage. Examples of this type of data include banking transactions, invoices, and customer records. Figure 1.18 shows the symbol used to represent structured data.

Unstructured Data

Data that does not conform to a data model or data schema is known as unstructured data. It is estimated that unstructured data makes up 80% of the data within any given enterprise. Unstructured data has a faster growth rate than structured data. Figure 1.19 illustrates some common types of unstructured data. This form of data is either textual or binary and often conveyed via files that are self-contained and non-relational. A text file may contain the contents of various tweets or blog postings. Binary files are often media files that contain image, audio or video data. Technically, both text and binary files have a structure defined by the file format itself, but this aspect is disregarded, and the notion of being unstructured is in relation to the format of the data contained in the file itself.

Figure 1.19

Video, image and audio files are all types of unstructured data.

video image files audio

Special purpose logic is usually required to process and store unstructured data. For example, to play a video file, it is essential that the correct codec (coder-decoder) is available. Unstructured data cannot be directly processed or queried using SQL. If it is required to be stored within a relational database, it is stored in a table as a Binary Large Object (BLOB). Alternatively, a Not-only SQL (NoSQL) database is a non-relational database that can be used to store unstructured data alongside structured data.

Semi-structured Data

Semi-structured data has a defined level of structure and consistency, but is not relational in nature. Instead, semi-structured data is hierarchical or graph-based. This kind of data is commonly stored in files that contain text. For instance, Figure 1.20 shows that XML and JSON files are common forms of semi-structured data. Due to the textual nature of this data and its conformance to some level of structure, it is more easily processed than unstructured data.

Examples of common sources of semi-structured data include electronic data interchange (EDI) files, spreadsheets, RSS feeds and sensor data. Semi-structured data often has special pre-processing and storage requirements, especially if the underlying format is not text-based. An example of pre-processing of semi-structured data would be the validation of an XML file to ensure that it conformed to its schema definition.

Figure 1.20
XML, JSON and sensor data
are semi-structured.

XML   JSON   sensor
data   data   data

Metadata

Metadata provides information about a dataset's characteristics and structure. This type of data is mostly machine-generated and can be appended to data. The tracking of metadata is crucial to Big Data processing, storage and analysis because it provides information about the pedigree of the data and its provenance during processing. Examples of metadata include:

Figure 1.21
The symbol used to
represent metadata.

- XML tags providing the author and creation date of a document

- attributes providing the file size and resolution of a digital photograph

Big Data solutions rely on metadata, particularly when processing semi-structured and unstructured data. Figure 1.21 shows the symbol used to represent metadata.

Case Study Background

Ensure to Insure (ETI) is a leading insurance company that provides a range of insurance plans in the health, building, marine and aviation sectors to its 25 million globally dispersed customer base. The company consists of a workforce of around 5,000 employees and generates annual revenue of more than 350,000,000 USD.

History

ETI started its life as an exclusive health insurance provider 50 years ago. As a result of multiple acquisitions over the past 30 years, ETI has extended its services to include property and casualty insurance plans in the building, marine and aviation sectors.

Each of its four sectors is comprised of a core team of specialized and experienced agents, actuaries, underwriters and claim adjusters.

The agents generate the company's revenue by selling policies while the actuaries are responsible for risk assessment, coming up with new insurance plans and revising existing plans. The actuaries also perform what-if analyses and make use of dashboards and scorecards for scenario evaluation. The underwriters evaluate new insurance applications and decide on the premium amount. The claim adjusters deal with investigating claims made against a policy and arrive at a settlement amount for the policyholder.

Some of the key departments within ETI include the underwriting, claims settlement, customer care, legal, marketing, human resource, accounts and IT departments. Both prospective and existing customers generally contact ETI's customer care department via telephone, although contact via email and social media has increased exponentially over the past few years.

ETI strives to distinguish itself by providing competitive policies and premium customer service that does not end once a policy has been sold. Its management believes that doing so helps to achieve increased levels of customer acquisition and retention. ETI relies heavily on its actuaries to create insurance plans that reflect the needs of its customers.

Technical Infrastructure and Automation Environment

ETI's IT environment consists of a combination of client-server and mainframe platforms that support the execution of a number of systems, including policy quotation, policy administration, claims management, risk assessment, document management, billing, enterprise resource planning (ERP) and customer relationship management (CRM).

The policy quotation system is used to create new insurance plans and to provide quotes to prospective customers. It is integrated with the website and customer care portal to provide website visitors and customer care agents the ability to obtain insurance quotes. The policy administration system handles all aspects of policy lifecycle management, including issuance, update, renewal and cancellation of policies. The claims management system deals with claim processing activities.

A claim is registered when a policyholder makes a report, which is then assigned to a claim adjuster who analyzes the claim in light of the available information that was submitted when the claim was made, as well other background information obtained from different internal and external sources. Based on the analyzed information, the claim is settled following a certain set of business rules. The risk assessment system is used by the actuaries to assess any potential risk, such as a storm or a flood that could result in policyholders making claims. The risk assessment system enables probability-based risk evaluation that involves executing various mathematical and statistical models.

The document management system serves as a central repository for all kinds of documents, including policies, claims, scanned documents and customer correspondence. The billing system keeps track of premium collection from customers and also generates various reminders for customers who have missed their payment via email and postal mail. The ERP system is used for day-to-day running of ETI, including human resource management and accounts. The CRM system records all aspects of customer communication via phone, email and postal mail and also provides a portal for call center agents for dealing with customer enquiries. Furthermore, it enables the marketing team to create, run and manage marketing campaigns. Data from these operational systems is exported to an Enterprise Data Warehouse (EDW) that is used to generate reports for financial and performance analysis. The EDW is also used to generate reports for different regulatory authorities to ensure continuous regulatory compliance.

Business Goals and Obstacles

Over the past few decades, the company's profitability has been in decline. A committee comprised of senior managers was formed to investigate and make recommendations. The committee's findings revealed that the main reason behind the company's deteriorating financial position is the increased number of fraudulent claims and the associated payments being made against them. These findings showed that the fraud committed has become complex and hard to detect because fraudsters have become more sophisticated and organized. Apart from incurring direct monetary loss, the costs related to the processing of fraudulent claims result in indirect loss.

Another contributing factor is a significant upsurge in the occurrence of catastrophes such as floods, storms and epidemics, which have also increased the number of high-end genuine claims. Further reasons for declines in revenue include customer defection due to slow claims processing and insurance products that no longer match the needs of customers. The latter weakness has been exposed by the emergence of tech-savvy competitors that employ the use of telematics to provide personalized policies.

The committee pointed out that the frequency with which the existing regulations change and new regulations are introduced has recently increased. The company has unfortunately been slow to respond and has not been able to ensure full and continuous compliance. Due to these shortcomings, ETI has had to pay heavy fines.

The committee noted that yet another reason behind the company's poor financial performance is that insurance plans are created and policies are underwritten without a thorough risk assessment. This has led to incorrect premiums being set and more payouts being made than anticipated. Currently, the shortfall between the collected premiums and the payouts made is compensated for with return on investments. However, this is not a long-term solution as it dilutes the profit made on investments. In addition, the insurance plans are generally based on the actuaries' experience and analysis of the population as a whole, resulting in insurance plans that only apply to an average set of customers. Customers whose circumstances deviate from the average set are not interested in such insurance plans.

The aforementioned reasons are also responsible for ETI's falling share price and decrease in market share.

Based on the committee's findings, the following strategic goals are set by ETI's directors:

1. Decrease losses by (a) improving risk evaluation and maximizing risk mitigation, which applies to both creation of insurance plans and when new applications are screened at the time of issuing a policy, (b) implementing a proactive catastrophe management system that decreases the number of potential claims resulting from a calamity and (c) detecting fraudulent claims.

2. Decrease customer defection and improve customer retention with (a) speedy settlement of claims and (b) personalized and competitive policies based on individual circumstances rather than demographic generalization alone.

3. Achieve and maintain full regulatory compliance at all times by employing enhanced risk management techniques that can better predict risks, because the majority of regulations require accurate knowledge of risks in order to ensure compliance.

After consulting with its IT team, the committee recommended the adoption of a data-driven strategy with enhanced analytics to be applied across multiple business functions in such a way that different business processes take into account relevant internal and external data. In this way, decisions can be based on evidence rather than on experience and intuition alone. In particular, augmentation of large amounts of structured data with large amounts of unstructured data is stressed in support of performing deep yet timely data analyses.

The committee asked the IT team if there are any existing obstacles that might prevent the implementation of the aforementioned strategy. The IT team was reminded of the financial constraints within which it needs to operate. In response to this, the team prepared a feasibility report that highlights the following obstacles:

- *Acquiring, storing and processing unstructured data from internal and external data sources* – Currently, only structured data is stored and processed, because the existing technology does not support the storage and processing of unstructured data.

- *Processing large amounts of data in a timely manner* – Although the EDW is used to generate reports based on historical data, the amount of data processed cannot be classified as large, and the reports take a long time to generate.

- *Processing multiple types of data and combining structured data with unstructured data* – Multiple types of unstructured data are produced, such as textual documents and call center logs that cannot currently be processed due to their unstructured nature. Secondly, structured data is used in isolation for all types of analyses.

The IT team concluded by issuing a recommendation that ETI adopt Big Data as the primary means of overcoming these impediments in support of achieving the set goals.

CASE STUDY EXAMPLE

Although ETI has chosen Big Data for the implementation of its strategic goals, as it currently stands, ETI has no in-house Big Data skills and needs to choose between hiring a Big Data consultant or sending its IT team on a Big Data training course. The latter option is chosen. However, only the senior IT team members are sent to the training in anticipation of a cost-effective, long-term solution where the trained team members will become a permanent in-house Big Data resource that can be consulted any time and can also train junior team members to further increase the in-house Big Data skillset.

Having received the Big Data training, the trained team members emphasize the need for a common vocabulary of terms so that the entire team is on the same page when talking about Big Data. An example-driven approach is adopted. When discussing datasets, some of the related datasets pointed out by the team members include claims, policies, quotes, customer profile data and census data. Although the data analysis and data analytics concepts are quickly comprehended, some of the team members that do not have much business exposure have trouble understanding BI and the establishment of appropriate KPIs. One of the trained IT team members explains BI by using the monthly report generation process for evaluating the previous month's performance as an example. This process involves importing data from operational systems into the EDW and generating KPIs such as policies sold and claims submitted, processed, accepted and rejected that are displayed on different dashboards and scorecards.

In terms of analytics, ETI makes use of both descriptive and diagnostic analytics. Descriptive analytics include querying the policy administration system to determine the number of polices sold each day, querying the claims management system to find out how many claims are submitted daily and querying the billing system to find out how many customers are behind on their premium payments. Diagnostic analytics are carried out as part of various BI activities, such as performing queries to answer questions such as why last month's sales target was not met. This includes performing drill-down operations to breakdown sales by type and location so that it can be determined which locations underperformed for specific types of policies.

ETI currently does not utilize predictive nor prescriptive analytics. However, the adoption of Big Data will enable it to perform these types of analytics as now it can make use of unstructured data, which when combined with structured data provides a rich resource in support of these analytics types. ETI has decided to implement these two types of analytics in a gradual manner by first implementing predictive analytics and then slowly building up their capabilities to implement prescriptive analytics.

At this stage, ETI is planning to make use of predictive analytics in support of achieving its goals. For example, predictive analytics will enable detection of fraudulent claims by predicting which claim is a fraudulent one and in case of customer defection by predicting which customers are likely to defect. In the future, via prescriptive analytics, it is anticipated that ETI can further enhance the realization of its goals. For example, prescriptive analytics can prescribe the correct premium amount considering all risk factors or can prescribe the best course of action to take for mitigating claims when faced with catastrophes, such as floods or storms.

Identifying Data Characteristics

The IT team members want to gauge different datasets that are generated inside ETI's boundary as well as any other data generated outside ETI's boundary that may be of interest to the company in the context of volume, velocity, variety, veracity and value characteristics. The team members take each characteristic in turn and discuss how different datasets manifest that characteristic.

Volume

The team notes that within the company, a large amount of transactional data is generated as a result of processing claims, selling new policies and changes to existing policies. However, a quick discussion reveals that large volumes of unstructured data, both inside and outside the company, may prove helpful in achieving ETI's goals. This data includes health records, documents submitted by the customers at the time of submitting an insurance application, property schedules, fleet data, social media data and weather data.

Velocity

With regards to the in-flow of data, some of the data is low velocity, such as the claims submission data and the new policies issued data. However, data such as webserver logs and insurance quotes is high velocity data. Looking outside the company, the IT team members anticipate that social media data and the weather data may arrive at a fast pace. Further, it is anticipated that for catastrophe management and fraudulent claim detection, data needs to be processed reasonably quickly to minimize losses.

Variety

In pursuit of its goals, ETI will be required to incorporate a range of datasets that include health records, policy data, claim data, quote data, social media data, call center agent notes, claim adjuster notes, incident photographs, weather reports, census data, webserver logs and emails.

Veracity

A sample of data taken from the operational systems and the EDW shows signs of high veracity. The IT team attributes this to the data validation performed at multiple stages including validation at the time of data entry, validation at various points when an application is processing data, such as function-level input validation, and validation performed by the database when data is persisted. Looking outside ETI's boundary, a study of a few samples taken from the social media data and weather data demonstrates further decline in veracity indicating that such data will require an increased level of data validation and cleansing to make it high veracity data.

Value

As far as the value characteristic is concerned, all IT team members concur that they need to draw maximum value out of the available datasets by ensuring the datasets are stored in their original form and that they are subjected to the right type of analytics.

Identifying Types of Data

The IT team members go through a categorization exercise of the various datasets that have been identified up until now and come up with the following list:

- Structured data: policy data, claim data, customer profile data and quote data.

- Unstructured data: social media data, insurance application documents, call center agent notes, claim adjuster notes and incident photographs.

- Semi-structured data: health records, customer profile data, weather reports, census data, webserver logs and emails.

Metadata is a new concept for the group as ETI's current data management procedures do not create nor append any metadata. Also, the current data processing practices do not take into account any metadata even if it were present. One of the reasons noted by the IT team is that currently, nearly all data that is stored and processed is structured in nature and originates from within the company. Hence, the origins and the characteristics of data are implicitly known. After some consideration, the members of the team realize that for the structured data, the data dictionary and the existence of last updated timestamp and last updated userid columns within the different relational database tables can be used as a form of metadata.

Chapter 2

Business Motivations and Drivers for Big Data Adoption

Marketplace Dynamics

Business Architecture

Business Process Management

Information and Communications Technology

Internet of Everything (IoE)

In many organizations it is now acceptable for a business to be architected in much the same way as its technology. This shift in perspective is reflected in the expanding domain of enterprise architecture, which used to be closely aligned with technology architecture but now includes business architecture as well. Although businesses still view themselves from a mechanistic system's point of view, with command and control being passed from executives to managers to front-line employees, feedback loops based upon linked and aligned measurements are providing greater insight into the effectiveness of management decision-making.

This cycle from decision to action to measurement and assessment of results creates opportunities for businesses to optimize their operations continuously. In fact, the mechanistic management view is being supplanted by one that is more organic and that drives the business based upon its ability to convert data into knowledge and insight. One problem with this perspective is that, traditionally, businesses were driven almost exclusively by internal data held in their information systems. However, companies are learning that this is not sufficient in order to execute their business models in a marketplace that more resembles an ecological system. As such, organizations need to consume data from the outside to sense directly the factors that influence their profitability. The use of such external data most often results in "Big Data" datasets.

This chapter explores the business motivations and drivers behind the adoption of Big Data solutions and technologies. The adoption of Big Data represents the confluence of several forces to include: marketplace dynamics, an appreciation and formalism of Business Architecture (BA), the realization that a business' ability to deliver value is directly tied to Business Process Management (BPM), innovation in Information and Communications Technology (ICT) and finally the Internet of Everything (IoE). Each of these topics will be explored in turn.

Marketplace Dynamics

There has been a fundamental shift in the way businesses view themselves and the marketplace. In the past 15 years, two large stock market corrections have taken place—the first was the dot-com bubble burst in 2000, and the second was the global recession that began in 2008. In each case, businesses entrenched and worked to improve their efficiency and effectiveness to stabilize their profitability by reducing costs. This of course is normal. When customers are scarce, cost-cutting often ensues to maintain the corporate bottom line. In this environment, companies conduct transformation projects to improve their corporate processes to achieve savings.

As the global economies began to emerge from recession, companies began to focus outward, looking to find new customers and keep existing customers from defecting to marketplace competitors. This was accomplished by offering new products and services and delivering increased value propositions to customers. It is a very different market cycle to the one that focuses on cost-cutting, for it is not about transformation but instead innovation. Innovation brings hope to a company that it will find new ways to achieve a competitive advantage in the marketplace and a consequent increase in top line revenue.

The global economy can experience periods of uncertainty due to various factors. We generally accept that the economies of the major developed countries in the world are now inextricably intertwined; in other words, they form a system of systems. Likewise, the world's businesses are shifting their perspective about their identity and independence as they recognize that they are also intertwined in intricate product and service networks.

For this reason, companies need to expand their Business Intelligence activities beyond retrospective reflection on internal information extracted from their corporate information systems. They need to open themselves to external data sources as a means of sensing the marketplace and their position within it. Recognizing that external data

Davenport and Prusak have provided generally-accepted working definitions of data, information and knowledge in their book *Working Knowledge*. According to Davenport and Prusak, "[d]ata is a set of discrete, objective facts about events." In a business sense, these events are activities that occur within an organization's business processes and information systems—they represent the generation, modification and completion of work associated with business entities; for example, orders, shipments, notifications and customer address updates. These events are a reflection of real-world activity that is represented within the relational data stores of corporate information systems. Davenport and Prusak further define information as "data that makes a difference." It is data that has been contextualized to provide communication; it delivers a message and informs the receiver—whether it be a human or system. Information is then enriched via experience and insight in the generation of knowledge. The authors state that "[k]nowledge is a fluid mix of framed experience, values, contextual information and expert insight that provides a framework for evaluating and incorporating new experiences and information."

brings additional context to their internal data allows a corporation to move up the analytic value chain from hindsight to insight with greater ease. With appropriate tooling, which often supports sophisticated simulation capabilities, a company can develop analytic results that provide foresight. In this case, the tooling assists in bridging the gap between knowledge and wisdom as well as provides advisory analytic results. This is the power of Big Data—enriching corporate perspective beyond introspection, from which a business can only infer information about marketplace sentiment, to sensing the marketplace itself.

The transition from hindsight to foresight can be understood through the lens of the DIKW pyramid depicted in Figure 2.1. Note that in this figure, at the top of the triangle, wisdom is shown as an outline to indicate that it exists but is not typically generated via ICT systems. Instead, knowledge workers provide the insight and experience to frame the available knowledge so that it can be integrated to form wisdom. Wisdom generation by technological means quickly devolves into a philosophical discussion that is not within the scope of this book. Within business environments, technology is used to support knowledge management, and personnel are responsible for applying their competency and wisdom to act accordingly.

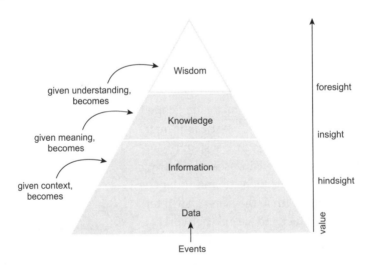

Figure 2.1
The DIKW pyramid shows how data can be enriched with context to create information, information can be supplied with meaning to create knowledge and knowledge can be integrated to form wisdom.

Business Architecture

Within the past decade, there has been a realization that too often a corporation's enterprise architecture is simply a myopic view of its technology architecture. In an effort to wrest power from the stronghold of IT, business architecture has emerged as a complementary discipline. In the future, the goal is that enterprise architecture will present a balanced view between business and technology architectures. Business architecture provides a means of blueprinting or concretely expressing the design of the business. A business architecture helps an organization align its strategic vision with its underlying execution, whether they be technical resources or human capital. Thus, a business architecture includes linkages from abstract concepts like business mission, vision, strategy and goals to more concrete ones like business services, organizational structure, key performance indicators and application services.

These linkages are important because they provide guidance as to how to align the business and its information technology. It is an accepted view that a business operates as a layered system—the top layer is the strategic layer occupied by C-level executives and advisory groups; the middle layer is the tactical or managerial layer that seeks to steer the organization in alignment with the strategy; and the bottom layer is the operations layer where a business executes its core processes and delivers value to its customers. These three layers often exhibit a degree of independence from one another, but each layer's goals and objectives are influenced by and often defined by the layer above, in other words top-down. From a monitoring perspective, communication flows upstream, or bottom-up via the collection of metrics. Business activity monitoring at the operations layer generates Performance Indicators (PIs) and metrics, for both services and processes. They are aggregated to create Key Performance Indicators (KPIs) used at the tactical layer. These KPIs can be aligned with Critical Success Factors (CSFs) at the strategic layer, which in turn help measure progress being made toward the achievement of strategic goals and objectives.

Big Data has ties to business architecture at each of the organizational layers, as depicted in Figure 2.2. Big Data enhances value as it provides additional context through the integration of external perspectives to help convert data into information and provide meaning to generate knowledge from information. For instance, at the operational level, metrics are generated that simply report on *what* is happening in the business. In essence, we are converting data through business concepts and context to generate information. At the managerial level, this information can be examined through the lens of corporate performance to answer questions regarding *how* the business is performing. In other words, give meaning to the information. This information may be further enriched to answer questions regarding *why* the business is performing at the level it is. When armed with this knowledge, the strategic layer can provide further insight to help answer questions of which strategy needs to change or be adopted in order to correct or enhance the performance.

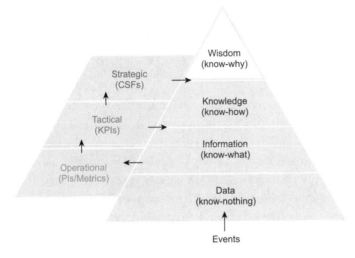

Figure 2.2
The DIKW pyramid illustrates alignment with Strategic, Tactical and Operational corporate levels.

As with any layered system, the layers do not all change at the same speed. In the case of a business enterprise, the strategic layer is the slowest moving layer, and the operational layer is the fastest moving layer. The slower moving layers provide stability and direction to the faster moving layers. In traditional organizational hierarchies, the management layer is responsible for directing the operational layer in alignment with the strategy created by the executive team. Because of this variation in regard to speed of change, it is possible to envision the three layers as being responsible for strategy execution, business execution and process execution respectively. Each of these layers relies upon different metrics and measures, presented through different visualization and reporting functions. For example, the strategy layer may rely upon balanced scorecards, the management layer upon an interactive visualization of KPIs and corporate performance and the operational layer on visualizations of executing business processes and their statuses.

Figure 2.3, a variant of a diagram produced by Joe Gollner in his blog post "The Anatomy of Knowledge," shows how an organization can relate and align its organizational layers by creating a virtuous cycle via a feedback loop. On the right side of the figure, the strategic layer drives response via the application of judgment by making decisions regarding corporate strategy, policy, goals and objectives that are communicated as constraints to the tactical layer. The tactical layer in turn leverages this knowledge to generate priorities and actions that conform to corporate direction. These actions adjust the execution of business at the operational layer. This in turn should generate measureable change in the experience of internal stakeholders and external customers as they deliver and consume business services. This change, or result, should surface and be visible in the data in the form of changed PIs that are then aggregated into KPIs. Recall that KPIs are metrics that can be associated with critical success factors that inform the executive team as to whether or not their strategies are working. Over time, the strategic and management layers injection of judgment and action into the loop will serve to refine the delivery of business services.

Figure 2.3
The creation of a virtuous cycle to align an organization across layers via a feedback loop.

Business Process Management

Businesses deliver value to customers and other stakeholders via the execution of their business processes. A business process is a description of how work is performed in an organization. It describes all work-related activities and their relationships, aligned with the organizational actors and resources responsible for conducting them. The relationships between activities may be temporal; for example, activity A is executed before activity B. The relationships can also describe whether the execution of activities is conditional, based upon the outputs or conditions generated by other activities or by sensing events generated outside of the business process itself.

Business process management applies process excellence techniques to improve corporate execution. Business Process Management Systems (BPMS) provide software developers a model driven platform that is becoming the Business Application Development Environment (BADE) of choice. A business application needs to: mediate between humans and other technology-hosted resources, execute in alignment with corporate policies and ensure the fair distribution of work to employees. As a BADE, models of a business process are joined with: models of organizational roles and structure, business entities and their relationships, business rules and the user-interface. The development environment integrates these models together to create a business application that manages screenflow and workflow and provides workload management. This is accomplished in an execution environment that enforces corporate policy and security and provides state management for long-running business processes. The state of an individual process, or all processes, can be interrogated via Business Activity Monitoring (BAM) and visualized.

When BPM is combined with BPMSs that are intelligent, processes can be executed in a goal-driven manner. Goals are connected to process fragments that are dynamically chosen and assembled at run-time in alignment with the evaluation of the goals. When the combination of Big Data analytic results and goal-driven behavior are used together, process execution can become adaptive to the marketplace and responsive to environmental conditions. As a simple example, a customer contact process has process fragments that enable communication with customers via a voice call, email, text message and traditional postal mail. In the beginning, the choice of these contact methods is unweighted, and they are chosen at random. However, behind-the-scenes analysis is being done to measure the effectiveness of the contact method via statistical analysis of customer responsiveness.

The results of this analysis are tied to a goal responsible for selecting the contact method, and when a clear preference is determined, the weighting is changed to favor the contact method that achieves the best response. A more detailed analysis could leverage customer clustering, which would assign individual customers to groups where one of the cluster dimensions is the contact method. In this case, customers can be contacted with even greater refinement, which provides a pathway to one-to-one targeted marketing.

Information and Communications Technology

This section examines the following ICT developments that have accelerated the pace of Big Data adoption in businesses:

- data analytics and data science
- digitization
- affordable technology and commodity hardware
- social media
- hyper-connected communities and devices
- cloud computing

Data Analytics and Data Science

Enterprises are collecting, procuring, storing, curating and processing increasing quantities of data. This is occurring in an effort to find new insights that can drive more efficient and effective operations, provide management the ability to steer the business proactively and allow the C-suite to better formulate and assess their strategic initiatives. Ultimately, enterprises are looking for new ways to gain a competitive edge. Thus the need for techniques and technologies that can extract meaningful information and insights has increased. Computational approaches, statistical techniques and data warehousing have advanced to the point where they have merged, each bringing their specific techniques and tools that allow the performance of Big Data analysis. The maturity of these fields of practice inspired and enabled much of the core functionality expected from contemporary Big Data solutions, environments and platforms.

Digitization

For many businesses, digital mediums have replaced physical mediums as the de facto communications and delivery mechanism. The use of digital artifacts saves both time and cost as distribution is supported by the vast pre-existing infrastructure of the Internet. As consumers connect to a business through their interaction with these digital substitutes, it leads to an opportunity to collect further "secondary" data; for example, requesting a customer to provide feedback, complete a survey, or simply providing a hook to display a relevant advertisement and tracking its click-through rate. Collecting secondary data can be important for businesses because mining this data can allow for customized marketing, automated recommendations and the development of optimized product features. Figure 2.4 provides a visual representation of examples of digitization.

Figure 2.4

Examples of digitization include online banking, on-demand television and streaming video.

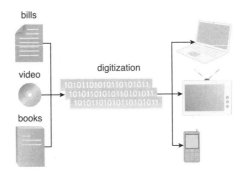

Affordable Technology and Commodity Hardware

Technology capable of storing and processing large quantities of diverse data has become increasingly affordable. Additionally, Big Data solutions often leverage open-source software that executes on commodity hardware, further reducing costs. The combination of commodity hardware and open source software has virtually eliminated the advantage that large enterprises used to hold by being able to outspend their smaller competitors due to the larger size of their IT budgets. Technology no longer delivers competitive advantage. Instead, it simply becomes the platform upon which the business executes. From a business standpoint, utilization of affordable technology and commodity hardware to generate analytic results that can further optimize the execution of its business processes is the path to competitive advantage.

The use of commodity hardware makes the adoption of Big Data solutions accessible to businesses without large capital investments. Figure 2.5 provides an example of the price decline associated with data storage prices over the past 20 years.

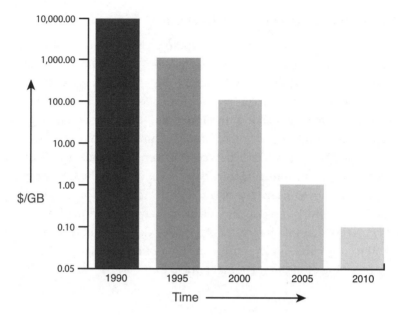

Figure 2.5

Data storage prices have dropped dramatically from more than $10,000 to less than $0.10 per GB over the decades.

Social Media

The emergence of social media has empowered customers to provide feedback in near-realtime via open and public mediums. This shift has forced businesses to consider customer feedback on their service and product offerings in their strategic planning. As a result, businesses are storing increasing amounts of data on customer interactions within their customer relationship management systems (CRM) and from harvesting customer reviews, complaints and praise from social media sites. This information feeds Big Data analysis algorithms that surface the voice of the customer in an attempt to provide better levels of service, increase sales, enable targeted marketing and even create new products and services. Businesses have realized that branding activity is no longer completely managed by internal marketing activities. Instead, product brands and corporate reputation are co-created by the company and its customers. For this reason, businesses are increasingly interested in incorporating publicly available datasets from social media and other external data sources.

Hyper-Connected Communities and Devices

The broadening coverage of the Internet and the proliferation of cellular and Wi-Fi networks has enabled more people and their devices to be continuously active in virtual communities. Coupled with the proliferation of Internet connected sensors, the underpinnings of the Internet of Things (IoT), a vast collection of smart Internet-connected devices, is being formed. As shown in Figure 2.6, this in turn has resulted in a massive increase in the number of available data streams. While some streams are public, other streams are channeled directly to corporations for analysis. As an example, the performance-based management contracts associated with heavy equipment used in the mining industry incentivize the optimal performance of preventive and predictive maintenance in an effort to reduce the need and avoid the downtime associated with unplanned corrective maintenance. This requires detailed analysis of sensor readings emitted by the equipment for the early detection of issues that can be resolved via the proactive scheduling of maintenance activities.

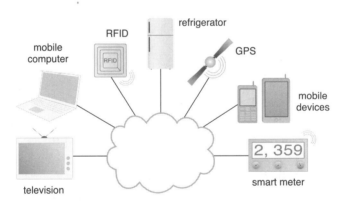

Figure 2.6

Hyper-connected communities and devices include television, mobile computing, RFIDs, refrigerators, GPS devices, mobile devices and smart meters.

Cloud Computing

Cloud computing advancements have led to the creation of environments that are capable of providing highly scalable, on-demand IT resources that can be leased via pay-as-you-go models. Businesses have the opportunity to leverage the infrastructure, storage and processing capabilities provided by these environments in order to build-out scalable Big Data solutions that can carry out large-scale processing tasks. Although traditionally thought of as off-premise environments typically depicted with a cloud symbol, businesses are also leveraging cloud management software to create on premise clouds to more effectively utilize their existing infrastructure via virtualization. In either case, the ability of a cloud to dynamically scale based upon load allows for the creation of resilient analytic environments that maximize efficient utilization of ICT resources.

Figure 2.7 displays an example of how a cloud environment can be leveraged for its scaling capabilities to perform Big Data processing tasks. The fact that off-premise cloud-based IT resources can be leased dramatically reduces the required up-front investment of Big Data projects.

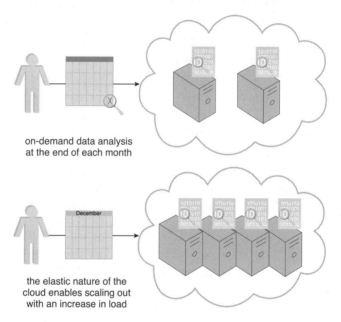

on-demand data analysis
at the end of each month

the elastic nature of the
cloud enables scaling out
with an increase in load

Figure 2.7
The cloud can be used to complete on-demand data analysis at the end of each month or enable the scaling out of systems with an increase in load.

It makes sense for enterprises already using cloud computing to reuse the cloud for their Big Data initiatives because:

- personnel already possesses the required cloud computing skills
- the input data already exists in the cloud

Migrating to the cloud is logical for enterprises planning to run analytics on datasets that are available via data markets, as many data markets make their datasets available in a cloud environment, such as Amazon S3.

In short, cloud computing can provide three essential ingredients required for a Big Data solution: external datasets, scalable processing capabilities and vast amounts of storage.

Internet of Everything (IoE)

The convergence of advancements in information and communications technology, marketplace dynamics, business architecture and business process management all contribute to the opportunity of what is now known as the Internet of Everything or IoE. The IoE combines the services provided by smart connected devices of the Internet of Things into meaningful business processes that possess the ability to provide unique and differentiating value propositions. It is a platform for innovation enabling the creation of new products and services and new sources of revenue for businesses. Big Data is the heart of the IoE. Hyper-connected communities and devices running on affordable technology and commodity hardware stream digitized data that is subject to analytic processes hosted in elastic cloud computing environments. The results of the analysis can provide insight as to how much value is generated by the current process and whether or not the process should proactively seek opportunities to further optimize itself.

IoE-specific companies can leverage Big Data to establish and optimize workflows and offer them to third parties as outsourced business processes. As established in the Business Process Manifesto edited by Roger Burlton (2011), an organization's business processes are the source for generating outcomes of value for customers and other stakeholders. In combination with the analysis of streaming data and customer context, being able to adapt the execution of these processes to align with the customer's goals will be a key corporate differentiator in the future.

One example of an area that has benefited from the IoE is precision agriculture, with traditional farming equipment manufacturers leading the way. When joined together as a system of systems, GPS-controlled tractors, in-field moisture and fertilization sensors, on-demand watering, fertilization, pesticide application systems and variable rate seeding equipment can maximize field productivity while minimizing cost. Precision agriculture enables alternative farming approaches that challenge industrial monoculture farms. With the aid of the IoE, smaller farms are able to compete by leveraging crop diversity and environmentally sensitive practices. Besides having smart connected farming equipment, the Big Data analysis of equipment and in-field sensor data can drive a decision support system that can guide farmers and their machines to optimum yields.

CASE STUDY EXAMPLE

ETI's committee of senior managers investigated the company's deteriorating financial position and realized that many of the corporation's current problems could have been detected earlier. If the management at the tactical level had greater awareness, they could have proactively taken action to avoid some of the losses. This lack of early warning was due to the fact that ETI failed to sense that marketplace dynamics had changed. New competitors using advanced technologies to process claims and set premiums had disrupted the market and taken a share of ETI's business. At the same time, the company's lack of sophisticated fraud detection has been exploited by unscrupulous customers and perhaps even organized crime.

The senior management team reports their findings to the executive management team. Subsequently, in light of the previous strategic goals that were established, a new set of transformation and innovation corporate priorities are established. These initiatives will be used to direct and guide corporate resources to solutions that will enhance ETI's ability to increase profits.

Considering transformation, business process management disciplines will be adopted to document, analyze and improve the processing of claims. These business process models will then be consumed by a Business Process Management System (BPMS), which is essentially a process automation framework, to ensure consistent and auditable process execution. This will help ETI demonstrate regulatory compliance. An additional benefit of using a BPMS is that the traceability of claims processed by the system includes information about which employees have processed which claim. Although it has not been confirmed, there is a suspicion that some portion of the fraudulent claims being processed may be traceable to employees that are subverting internal manual controls driven by corporate policy. In other words, not only will the BPMS enhance the ability to meet external regulatory compliance, it will also enforce standard operating procedures and work practices within ETI.

Risk assessment and fraud detection will be enhanced with the application of innovative Big Data technologies that will produce analytic results that can drive data-driven decision-making. The risk assessment results will help actuaries lessen their reliance on intuition by providing them with generated risk assessment metrics. Furthermore, the output of the fraud detection capability will be incorporated into the automated claims processing workflow. The fraud detection results will also be used to direct questionable claims to experienced claims adjustors. The adjustors will be able to more carefully assess the nature of a claim in relation to ETI claim liability and the likelihood of it actually being fraudulent. Over time, this manual processing could lead to greater automation as the claims adjusters' decisions are tracked by the BPMS and can therefore be used to create training sets of claims data that include the decision of whether or not the claim was deemed fraudulent. These training sets will enhance ETI's ability to perform predictive analytics, for the sets can be consumed by an automated classifier.

Of course, the executives also realize that they have been unable to continuously optimize the operations of ETI because they have not been enriching data sufficiently enough to generate knowledge. The reason for this is ultimately traced to a lack of understanding of business architecture. Corporately, the executives realize that they have been treating every measurement as a Key Performance Indicator (KPI). This has generated lots of analysis, but since it lacked focus, it was not delivering on its potential value. With the realization that KPIs are higher-level metrics and fewer in quantity, they were able to readily agree on the handful of metrics that should be monitored at the tactical level.

Additionally, the executives have always had trouble aligning business execution with strategic execution. This was caused in part by a failure to define Critical Success Factors (CSFs). Strategic goals and objectives should be assessed by CSFs rather than KPIs. Putting CSFs in place has helped ETI link and align the strategic, tactical and operating levels of their business. The executive and management teams will be closely monitoring their new measurement and assessment initiative in an effort to quantify the benefits it delivers over the next quarter.

One final decision was made by the executives at ETI. This decision created a new organizational role responsible for innovation management. The executives realized that the company had become too introspective. Caught up in the work of managing four insurance product lines, the team failed to recognize that the marketplace was changing. The group was surprised to learn about the benefits of Big Data and contemporary data analytics tools and technologies. Likewise, although they had digitized their e-billing and made heavy use of scanning technologies for claims processing, they had not considered that customer use of smartphone technology could produce new channels of digital information that could further streamline claims processing. Although the executives do not feel that they are in a position to adopt cloud technology at the infrastructure level, they have considered using third-party software as a service provider to reduce the operational costs associated with managing their relationship with customers.

At this point, the executive and senior management teams believe that they have addressed organizational alignment issues, put a plan in place to adopt business process management disciplines and technology, and successfully adopted Big Data, which will increase their ability to sense the marketplace and therefore be better able to adapt to changing conditions.

Chapter 3

Big Data Adoption and Planning Considerations

Big Data initiatives are strategic in nature and should be business-driven. The adoption of Big Data can be transformative but is more often innovative. Transformation activities are typically low-risk endeavors designed to deliver increased efficiency and effectiveness. Innovation requires a shift in mindset because it will fundamentally alter the structure of a business either in its products, services or organization. This is the power of Big Data adoption; it can enable this sort of change. Innovation management requires care—too many controlling forces can stifle the initiative and dampen the results, and too little oversight can turn a best intentioned project into a science experiment that never delivers promised results. It is against this backdrop that Chapter 3 addresses Big Data adoption and planning considerations.

Given the nature of Big Data and its analytic power, there are many issues that need to be considered and planned for in the beginning. For example, with the adoption of any new technology, the means to secure it in a way that conforms to existing corporate standards needs to be addressed. Issues related to tracking the provenance of a dataset from its procurement to its utilization is often a new requirement for organizations. Managing the privacy of constituents whose data is being handled or whose identity is revealed by analytic processes must be planned for. Big Data even opens up additional opportunities to consider moving beyond on-premise environments and into remotely-provisioned, scalable environments that are hosted in a cloud. In fact, all of the above considerations require an organization to recognize and establish a set of distinct governance processes and decision frameworks to ensure that responsible parties understand Big Data's nature, implications and management requirements.

Organizationally, the adoption of Big Data changes the approach to performing business analytics. For this reason, a Big Data analytics lifecycle is introduced in this chapter. The lifecycle begins with the establishment of a business case for the Big Data project and ends with ensuring that the analytic results are deployed to the organization to generate maximal value. There are a number of stages in between that organize the steps of identifying, procuring, filtering, extracting, cleansing and aggregating of data. This is all required before the analysis even occurs. The execution of this lifecycle requires new competencies to be developed or hired into the organization.

As demonstrated, there are many things to consider and account for when adopting Big Data. This chapter explains the primary potential issues and considerations.

Organization Prerequisites

Big Data frameworks are not turn-key solutions. In order for data analysis and analytics to offer value, enterprises need to have data management and Big Data governance frameworks. Sound processes and sufficient skillsets for those who will be responsible for implementing, customizing, populating and using Big Data solutions are also necessary. Additionally, the quality of the data targeted for processing by Big Data solutions needs to be assessed.

Outdated, invalid, or poorly identified data will result in low-quality input which, regardless of how good the Big Data solution is, will continue to produce low-quality results. The longevity of the Big Data environment also needs to be planned for. A roadmap needs to be defined to ensure that any necessary expansion or augmentation of the environment is planned out to stay in sync with the requirements of the enterprise.

Data Procurement

The acquisition of Big Data solutions themselves can be economical, due to the availability of open-source platforms and tools and opportunities to leverage commodity hardware. However, a substantial budget may still be required to obtain external data. The nature of the business may make external data very valuable. The greater the volume and variety of data that can be supplied, the higher the chances are of finding hidden insights from patterns.

External data sources include government data sources and commercial data markets. Government-provided data, such as geo-spatial data, may be free. However, most commercially relevant data will need to be purchased and may involve the continuation of subscription costs to ensure the delivery of updates to procured datasets.

Privacy

Performing analytics on datasets can reveal confidential information about organizations or individuals. Even analyzing separate datasets that contain seemingly benign data can reveal private information when the datasets are analyzed jointly. This can lead to intentional or inadvertent breaches of privacy.

Addressing these privacy concerns requires an understanding of the nature of data being accumulated and relevant data privacy regulations, as well as special techniques for data tagging and anonymization. For example, telemetry data, such as a car's GPS log or smart meter data readings, collected over an extended period of time can reveal an individual's location and behavior, as shown in Figure 3.1.

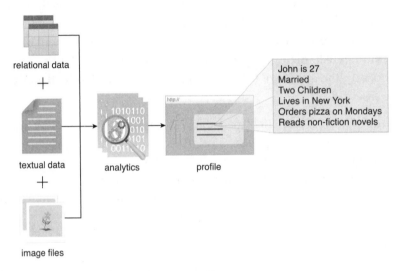

relational data

+

textual data

+

image files

analytics

profile

John is 27
Married
Two Children
Lives in New York
Orders pizza on Mondays
Reads non-fiction novels

Figure 3.1

Information gathered from running analytics on image files, relational data and textual data is used to create John's profile.

Security

Some of the components of Big Data solutions lack the robustness of traditional enterprise solution environments when it comes to access control and data security. Securing Big Data involves ensuring that the data networks and repositories are sufficiently secured via authentication and authorization mechanisms.

Big Data security further involves establishing data access levels for different categories of users. For example, unlike traditional relational database management systems, NoSQL databases generally do not provide robust built-in security mechanisms. They instead rely on simple HTTP-based APIs where data is exchanged in plaintext, making the data prone to network-based attacks, as shown in Figure 3.2.

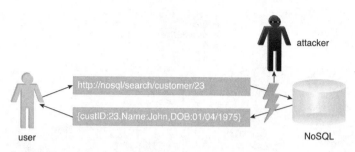

Figure 3.2
NoSQL databases can be susceptible to network-based attacks.

Provenance

Provenance refers to information about the source of the data and how it has been processed. Provenance information helps determine the authenticity and quality of data, and it can be used for auditing purposes. Maintaining provenance as large volumes of data are acquired, combined and put through multiple processing stages can be a complex task. At different stages in the analytics lifecycle, data will be in different states due to the fact it may be being transmitted, processed or in storage. These states correspond to the notion of data-in-motion, data-in-use and data-at-rest. Importantly, whenever Big Data changes state, it should trigger the capture of provenance information that is recorded as metadata.

As data enters the analytic environment, its provenance record can be initialized with the recording of information that captures the pedigree of the data. Ultimately, the goal of capturing provenance is to be able to reason over the generated analytic results with the knowledge of the origin of the data and what steps or algorithms were used to process the data that led to the result. Provenance information is essential to being able to realize the value of the analytic result. Much like scientific research, if results cannot be justified and repeated, they lack credibility. When provenance information is captured on the way to generating analytic results as in Figure 3.3, the results can be more easily trusted and thereby used with confidence.

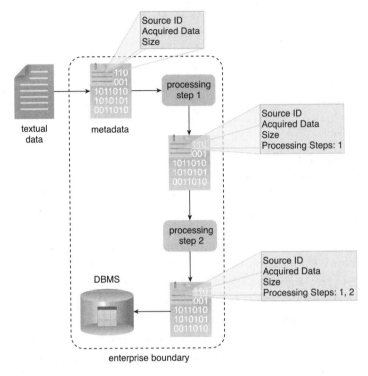

Figure 3.3

Data may also need to be annotated with source dataset attributes and processing step details as it passes through the data transformation steps.

Limited Realtime Support

Dashboards and other applications that require streaming data and alerts often demand realtime or near-realtime data transmissions. Many open source Big Data solutions and tools are batch-oriented; however, there is a new generation of realtime capable open source tools that have support for streaming data analysis. Many of the realtime data analysis solutions that do exist are proprietary. Approaches that achieve near-realtime results often process transactional data as it arrives and combine it with previously summarized batch-processed data.

Distinct Performance Challenges

Due to the volumes of data that some Big Data solutions are required to process, performance is often a concern. For example, large datasets coupled with complex search algorithms can lead to long query times. Another performance challenge is related to network bandwidth. With increasing data volumes, the time to transfer a unit of data can exceed its actual data processing time, as shown in Figure 3.4.

Figure 3.4
Transferring 1 PB of data via a 1-Gigabit LAN connection at 80% throughput will take approximately 2,750 hours.

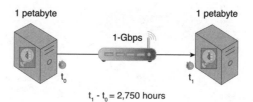

1 petabyte   1-Gbps   1 petabyte

t_0 t_1

$t_1 - t_0 = 2{,}750$ hours

Distinct Governance Requirements

Big Data solutions access data and generate data, all of which become assets of the business. A governance framework is required to ensure that the data and the solution environment itself are regulated, standardized and evolved in a controlled manner.

Examples of what a Big Data governance framework can encompass include:

- standardization of how data is tagged and the metadata used for tagging
- policies that regulate the kind of external data that may be acquired
- policies regarding the management of data privacy and data anonymization
- policies for the archiving of data sources and analysis results
- policies that establish guidelines for data cleansing and filtering

Distinct Methodology

A methodology will be required to control how data flows into and out of Big Data solutions. It will need to consider how feedback loops can be established to enable the processed data to undergo repeated refinement, as shown in Figure 3.5. For example, an iterative approach may be used to enable business personnel to provide IT personnel with feedback on a periodic basis. Each feedback cycle provides opportunities for system refinement by modifying data preparation or data analysis steps.

Figure 3.5

Each repetition can help
fine-tune processing steps,
algorithms and data models
to improve the accuracy of
results and deliver greater
value to the business.

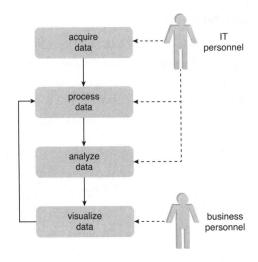

Clouds

As mentioned in Chapter 2, clouds provide remote environments that can host IT infrastructure for large-scale storage and processing, among other things. Regardless of
whether an organization is already cloud-enabled, the adoption of a Big Data environment may necessitate that some or all of that environment be hosted within a cloud. For
example, an enterprise that runs its CRM system in a cloud decides to add a Big Data
solution in the same cloud environment in order to run analytics on its CRM data. This
data can then be shared with its primary Big Data environment that resides within the
enterprise boundaries.

Common justifications for incorporating a cloud environment in support of a Big Data
solution include:

- inadequate in-house hardware resources

- upfront capital investment for system procurement is not available

- the project is to be isolated from the rest of the business so that existing business
  processes are not impacted

- the Big Data initiative is a proof of concept

- datasets that need to be processed are already cloud resident

- the limits of available computing and storage resources used by an in-house
  Big Data solution are being reached

Big Data Analytics Lifecycle

Big Data analysis differs from traditional data analysis primarily due to the volume, velocity and variety characteristics of the data being processes. To address the distinct requirements for performing analysis on Big Data, a step-by-step methodology is needed to organize the activities and tasks involved with acquiring, processing, analyzing and repurposing data. The upcoming sections explore a specific data analytics lifecycle that organizes and manages the tasks and activities associated with the analysis of Big Data. From a Big Data adoption and planning perspective, it is important that in addition to the lifecycle, consideration be made for issues of training, education, tooling and staffing of a data analytics team.

The Big Data analytics lifecycle can be divided into the following nine stages, as shown in Figure 3.6:

1. Business Case Evaluation
2. Data Identification
3. Data Acquisition & Filtering
4. Data Extraction
5. Data Validation & Cleansing
6. Data Aggregation & Representation
7. Data Analysis
8. Data Visualization
9. Utilization of Analysis Results

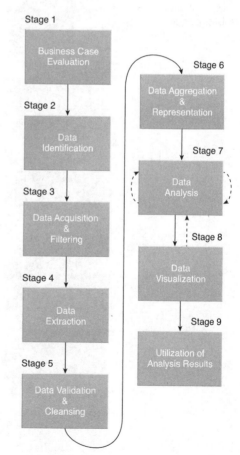

Figure 3.6

The nine stages of the Big Data analytics lifecycle.

Business Case Evaluation

Each Big Data analytics lifecycle must begin with a well-defined business case that presents a clear understanding of the justification, motivation and goals of carrying out the analysis. The Business Case Evaluation stage shown in Figure 3.7 requires that a business case be created, assessed and approved prior to proceeding with the actual hands-on analysis tasks.

An evaluation of a Big Data analytics business case helps decision-makers understand the business resources that will need to be utilized and which business challenges the analysis will tackle. The further identification of KPIs during this stage can help determine assessment criteria and guidance for the evaluation of the analytic results. If KPIs

Figure 3.7

Stage 1 of the Big Data analytics lifecycle.

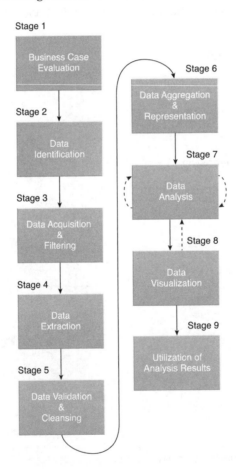

are not readily available, efforts should be made to make the goals of the analysis project SMART, which stands for specific, measurable, attainable, relevant and timely.

Based on business requirements that are documented in the business case, it can be determined whether the business problems being addressed are really Big Data problems. In order to qualify as a Big Data problem, a business problem needs to be directly related to one or more of the Big Data characteristics of volume, velocity, or variety.

Note also that another outcome of this stage is the determination of the underlying budget required to carry out the analysis project. Any required purchase, such as tools, hardware and training, must be understood in advance so that the anticipated investment can be weighed against the expected benefits of achieving the goals. Initial iterations of the Big Data analytics lifecycle will require more up-front investment of Big Data technologies, products and training compared to later iterations where these earlier investments can be repeatedly leveraged.

Data Identification

The Data Identification stage shown in Figure 3.8 is dedicated to identifying the datasets required for the analysis project and their sources.

Identifying a wider variety of data sources may increase the probability of finding hidden patterns and correlations. For example, to provide insight, it can be beneficial to identify as many types of related data sources as possible, especially when it is unclear exactly what to look for.

Depending on the business scope of the analysis project and nature of the business problems being addressed, the required datasets and their sources can be internal and/or external to the enterprise.

In the case of internal datasets, a list of available datasets from internal sources, such as data marts and operational systems, are typically compiled and matched against a pre-defined dataset specification.

In the case of external datasets, a list of possible third-party data providers, such as data markets and publicly available datasets, are compiled. Some forms of external data may be embedded within blogs or other types of content-based web sites, in which case they may need to be harvested via automated tools.

Figure 3.8

Data Identification is stage 2 of the Big Data analytics lifecycle.

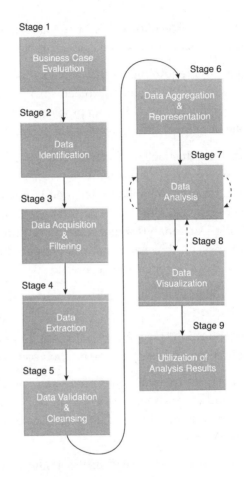

Data Acquisition and Filtering

During the Data Acquisition and Filtering stage, shown in Figure 3.9, the data is gathered from all of the data sources that were identified during the previous stage. The acquired data is then subjected to automated filtering for the removal of corrupt data or data that has been deemed to have no value to the analysis objectives.

Depending on the type of data source, data may come as a collection of files, such as data purchased from a third-party data provider, or may require API integration, such as with Twitter. In many cases, especially where external, unstructured data is concerned, some or most of the acquired data may be irrelevant (noise) and can be discarded as part of the filtering process.

Figure 3.9

Stage 3 of the Big Data analytics lifecycle.

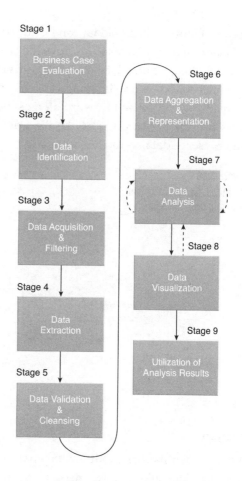

Data classified as "corrupt" can include records with missing or nonsensical values or invalid data types. Data that is filtered out for one analysis may possibly be valuable for a different type of analysis. Therefore, it is advisable to store a verbatim copy of the original dataset before proceeding with the filtering. To minimize the required storage space, the verbatim copy can be compressed.

Both internal and external data needs to be persisted once it gets generated or enters the enterprise boundary. For batch analytics, this data is persisted to disk prior to analysis. In the case of realtime analytics, the data is analyzed first and then persisted to disk.

As evidenced in Figure 3.10, metadata can be added via automation to data from both internal and external data sources to improve the classification and querying. Examples of appended metadata include dataset size and structure, source information, date and time of creation or collection and language-specific information. It is vital that metadata be machine-readable and passed forward along subsequent analysis stages. This helps maintain data provenance throughout the Big Data analytics lifecycle, which helps to establish and preserve data accuracy and quality.

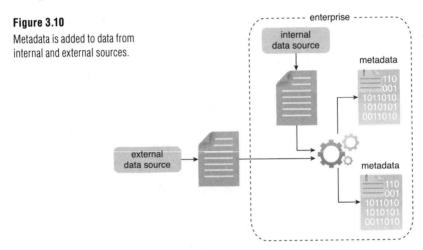

Figure 3.10

Metadata is added to data from internal and external sources.

Data Extraction

Some of the data identified as input for the analysis may arrive in a format incompatible with the Big Data solution. The need to address disparate types of data is more likely with data from external sources. The Data Extraction lifecycle stage, shown in Figure 3.11, is dedicated to extracting disparate data and transforming it into a format that the underlying Big Data solution can use for the purpose of the data analysis.

The extent of extraction and transformation required depends on the types of analytics and capabilities of the Big Data solution. For example, extracting the required fields from delimited textual data, such as with webserver log files, may not be necessary if the underlying Big Data solution can already directly process those files.

Similarly, extracting text for text analytics, which requires scans of whole documents, is simplified if the underlying Big Data solution can directly read the document in its native format.

Figure 3.12 illustrates the extraction of comments and a user ID embedded within an XML document without the need for further transformation.

Figure 3.11
Stage 4 of the Big Data analytics lifecycle.

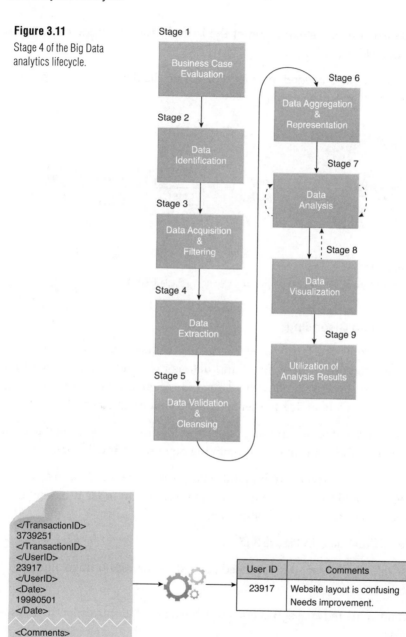

Stage 1
Business Case Evaluation

Stage 2
Data Identification

Stage 3
Data Acquisition & Filtering

Stage 4
Data Extraction

Stage 5
Data Validation & Cleansing

Stage 6
Data Aggregation & Representation

Stage 7
Data Analysis

Stage 8
Data Visualization

Stage 9
Utilization of Analysis Results

```
</TransactionID>
3739251
</TransactionID>
</UserID>
23917
</UserID>
<Date>
19980501
</Date>

<Comments>
Website layout is confusing
Needs improvement.
</Comments>
```

User ID	Comments
23917	Website layout is confusing Needs improvement.

Figure 3.12
Comments and user IDs are extracted from an XML document.

Figure 3.13 demonstrates the extraction of the latitude and longitude coordinates of a user from a single JSON field.

Further transformation is needed in order to separate the data into two separate fields as required by the Big Data solution.

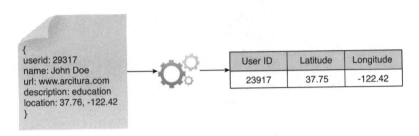

Figure 3.13
The user ID and coordinates of a user are extracted from a single JSON field.

Data Validation and Cleansing

Invalid data can skew and falsify analysis results. Unlike traditional enterprise data, where the data structure is pre-defined and data is pre-validated, data input into Big Data analyses can be unstructured without any indication of validity. Its complexity can further make it difficult to arrive at a set of suitable validation constraints.

The Data Validation and Cleansing stage shown in Figure 3.14 is dedicated to establishing often complex validation rules and removing any known invalid data.

Big Data solutions often receive redundant data across different datasets. This redundancy can be exploited to explore interconnected datasets in order to assemble validation parameters and fill in missing valid data.

For example, as illustrated in Figure 3.15:

- The first value in Dataset B is validated against its corresponding value in Dataset A.

- The second value in Dataset B is not validated against its corresponding value in Dataset A.

- If a value is missing, it is inserted from Dataset A.

Figure 3.14

Stage 5 of the Big Data
analytics lifecycle.

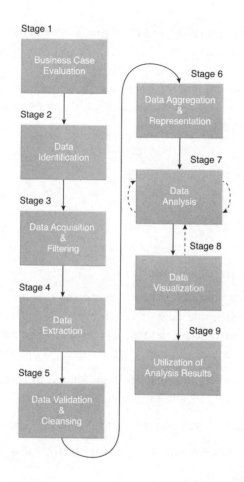

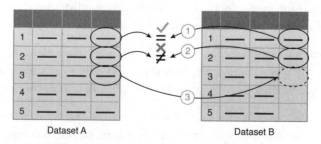

Dataset A   Dataset B

Figure 3.15

Data validation can be used to examine interconnected datasets in order
to fill in missing valid data.

For batch analytics, data validation and cleansing can be achieved via an offline ETL operation. For realtime analytics, a more complex in-memory system is required to validate and cleanse the data as it arrives from the source. Provenance can play an important role in determining the accuracy and quality of questionable data. Data that appears to be invalid may still be valuable in that it may possess hidden patterns and trends, as shown in Figure 3.16.

Figure 3.16

The presence of invalid data is resulting in spikes. Although the data appears abnormal, it may be indicative of a new pattern.

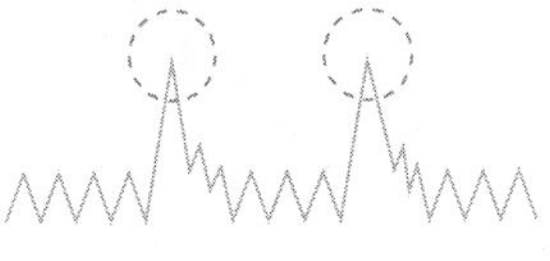

Data Aggregation and Representation

Data may be spread across multiple datasets, requiring that datasets be joined together via common fields, for example date or ID. In other cases, the same data fields may appear in multiple datasets, such as date of birth. Either way, a method of data reconciliation is required or the dataset representing the correct value needs to be determined.

The Data Aggregation and Representation stage, shown in Figure 3.17, is dedicated to integrating multiple datasets together to arrive at a unified view.

Performing this stage can become complicated because of differences in:

- *Data Structure* – Although the data format may be the same, the data model may be different.

- *Semantics* – A value that is labeled differently in two different datasets may mean the same thing, for example "surname" and "last name."

The large volumes processed by Big Data solutions can make data aggregation a time and effort-intensive operation. Reconciling these differences can require complex logic that is executed automatically without the need for human intervention.

Future data analysis requirements need to be considered during this stage to help foster data reusability. Whether data aggregation is required or not, it is important to understand that the same data can be stored in many different forms. One form may be better suited for a particular type of analysis than another. For example, data stored as a BLOB would be of little use if the analysis requires access to individual data fields.

Figure 3.17

Stage 6 of the Big Data analytics lifecycle.

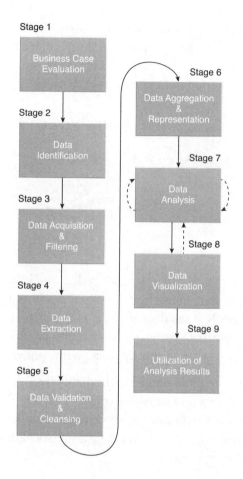

A data structure standardized by the Big Data solution can act as a common denominator that can be used for a range of analysis techniques and projects. This can require establishing a central, standard analysis repository, such as a NoSQL database, as shown in Figure 3.18.

Figure 3.18

A simple example of data aggregation where two datasets are aggregated together using the Id field.

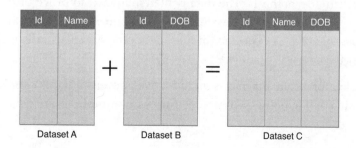

Figure 3.19 shows the same piece of data stored in two different formats. Dataset A contains the desired piece of data, but it is part of a BLOB that is not readily accessible for querying. Dataset B contains the same piece of data organized in column-based storage, enabling each field to be queried individually.

Figure 3.19

Dataset A and B can
be combined to create
a standardized data
structure with a Big Data
solution.

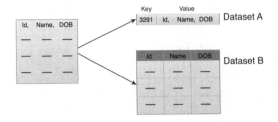

Data Analysis

The Data Analysis stage shown in Figure 3.20 is dedicated to carrying out the actual analysis task, which typically involves one or more types of analytics. This stage can be iterative in nature, especially if the data analysis is exploratory, in which case analysis is repeated until the appropriate pattern or correlation is uncovered. The exploratory analysis approach will be explained shortly, along with confirmatory analysis.

Depending on the type of analytic result required, this stage can be as simple as querying a dataset to compute an aggregation for comparison. On the other hand, it can be as challenging as combining data mining and complex statistical analysis techniques to discover patterns and anomalies or to generate a statistical or mathematical model to depict relationships between variables.

Data analysis can be classified as confirmatory analysis or exploratory analysis, the latter of which is linked to data mining, as shown in Figure 3.21.

Confirmatory data analysis is a deductive approach where the cause of the phenomenon being investigated is proposed beforehand. The proposed cause or assumption is called a hypothesis. The data is then analyzed to prove or disprove the hypothesis and provide definitive answers to specific questions. Data sampling techiniques are typically used. Unexpected findings or anomalies are usually ignored since a predetermined cause was assumed.

Exploratory data analysis is an inductive approach that is closely associated with data mining. No hypothesis or predetermined assumptions are generated. Instead, the data

Figure 3.20

Stage 7 of the Big Data
analytics lifecycle.

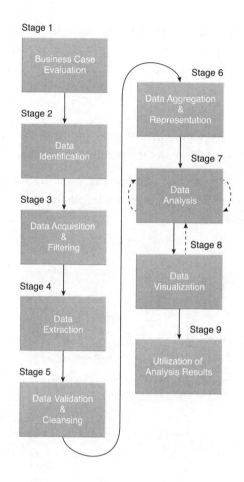

Figure 3.21

Data analysis can be carried
out as confirmatory or
exploratory analysis.

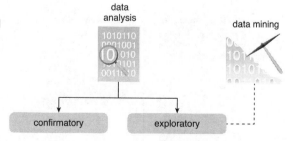

is explored through analysis to develop an understanding of the cause of the phenomenon. Although it may not provide definitive answers, this method provides a general direction that can facilitate the discovery of patterns or anomalies.

Data Visualization

The ability to analyze massive amounts of data and find useful insights carries little value if the only ones that can interpret the results are the analysts.

The Data Visualization stage, shown in Figure 3.22, is dedicated to using data visualization techniques and tools to graphically communicate the analysis results for effective interpretation by business users.

Figure 3.22

Stage 8 of the Big Data analytics lifecycle.

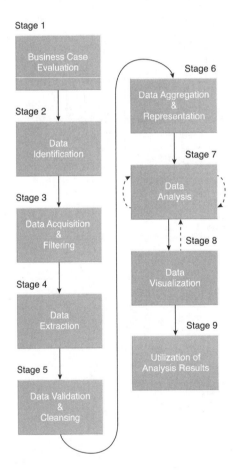

Business users need to be able to understand the results in order to obtain value from the analysis and subsequently have the ability to provide feedback, as indicated by the dashed line leading from stage 8 back to stage 7.

The results of completing the Data Visualization stage provide users with the ability to perform visual analysis, allowing for the discovery of answers to questions that users have not yet even formulated. Visual analysis techniques are covered later in this book.

The same results may be presented in a number of different ways, which can influence the interpretation of the results. Consequently, it is important to use the most suitable visualization technique by keeping the business domain in context.

Another aspect to keep in mind is that providing a method of drilling down to comparatively simple statistics is crucial, in order for users to understand how the rolled up or aggregated results were generated.

Utilization of Analysis Results

Subsequent to analysis results being made available to business users to support business decision-making, such as via dashboards, there may be further opportunities to utilize the analysis results. The Utilization of Analysis Results stage, shown in Figure 3.23, is dedicated to determining how and where processed analysis data can be further leveraged.

Depending on the nature of the analysis problems being addressed, it is possible for the analysis results to produce "models" that encapsulate new insights and understandings about the nature of the patterns and relationships that exist within the data that was analyzed. A model may look like a mathematical equation or a set of rules. Models can be used to improve business process logic and application system logic, and they can form the basis of a new system or software program.

Common areas that are explored during this stage include the following:

- *Input for Enterprise Systems* – The data analysis results may be automatically or manually fed directly into enterprise systems to enhance and optimize their behaviors and performance. For example, an online store can be fed processed customer-related analysis results that may impact how it generates product recommendations. New models may be used to improve the programming logic within existing enterprise systems or may form the basis of new systems.

- *Business Process Optimization* – The identified patterns, correlations and anomalies discovered during the data analysis are used to refine business processes. An example is consolidating transportation routes as part of a supply chain process. Models may also lead to opportunities to improve business process logic.

- *Alerts* – Data analysis results can be used as input for existing alerts or may form the basis of new alerts. For example, alerts may be created to inform users via email or SMS text about an event that requires them to take corrective action.

Figure 3.23

Stage 9 of the Big Data analytics lifecycle.

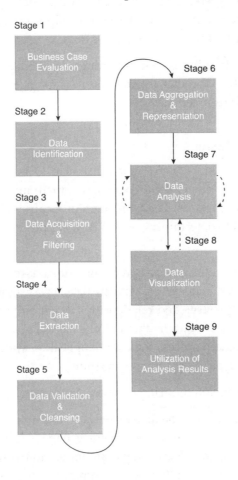

CASE STUDY EXAMPLE

The majority of ETI's IT team is convinced that Big Data is the silver bullet that will address all of their current issues. However, the trained IT members point out that adopting Big Data is not the same as simply adopting a technology platform. Rather, a range of factors first need to be considered in order to ensure successful adoption of Big Data. Therefore, to ensure that the impact of business-related factors is fully understood, the IT team sits together with the business managers to create a feasibility report. Involving business personnel at this early stage will further help create an environment that reduces the gap between management's perceived expectations and what IT can actually deliver.

There is a strong understanding that the adoption of Big Data is business-oriented and will assist ETI in reaching its goals. Big Data's abilities to store and process large amounts of unstructured data and combine multiple datasets will help ETI comprehend risk. The company hopes that, as a result, it can minimize losses by only accepting less-risky applicants as customers. Similarly, ETI predicts that the ability to look into the unstructured behavioral data of a customer and discover abnormal behavior will further help reduce loss because fraudulent claims can be rejected.

The decision to train the IT team in the field of Big Data has increased ETI's readiness for adopting Big Data. The team believes that it now has the basic skillset required for undertaking a Big Data initiative. Data identified and categorized earlier puts the team in a strong position for deciding on the required technologies. The early engagement of business management has also provided insights that allow them to anticipate changes that may be required in the future to keep the Big Data solution platform in alignment with any emerging business requirements.

At this preliminary stage, only a handful of external data sources, such as social media and census data, have been identified. It is agreed by the business personnel that a sufficient budget will be allocated for the acquisition of data from third-party data providers. Regarding privacy, the business users are a bit wary that obtaining additional data about customers could spark customer distrust. However, it is thought that an incentive-driven scheme, such as lower premiums, can be introduced in order to gain customers' consent and trust. When considering issues of security, the IT team notes that additional development efforts will be required to ensure that standardized, role-based access controls are in place for data held within the Big Data solution environment. This is especially relevant for the open-source databases that will hold non-relational data.

Although the business users are excited about being able to perform deep analytics through the use of unstructured data, they pose a question regarding the degree to which can they trust the results, for the analysis involves data from third-party data providers. The IT team responds that a framework will be adopted for adding and updating metadata for each dataset that is stored and processed so that provenance is maintained at all times and processing results can be traced all the way back to the constituent data sources.

ETI's present goals include decreasing the time it takes to settle claims and detect fraudulent claims. The achievement of these goals will require a solution that provides results in a timely manner. However, it is not anticipated that realtime data analysis support will be required. The IT team believes that these goals can be satisfied by developing a batch-based Big Data solution that leverages open source Big Data technology.

ETI's current IT infrastructure consists of comparatively older networking standards. Similarly, the specifications of most of the servers, such as the processor speed, disk capacity and disk speed, dictate that they are not capable of providing optimum data processing performance. Hence it is agreed that the current IT infrastructure needs an upgrade before a Big Data solution can be designed and built.

Both the business and IT teams strongly believe that a Big Data governance framework is required to not only help them standardize the usage of disparate data sources but also fully comply with any data privacy-related regulations. Furthermore, due to the business focus of the data analysis and to ensure that meaningful analysis results are generated, it is decided that an iterative data analysis approach that includes business personnel from the relevant department needs to be adopted. For example, in the "improving customer retention" scenario, the marketing and sales team can be included in the data analysis process right from the selection of datasets so that only the relevant attributes of these datasets are chosen. Later, the business team can provide valuable feedback in terms of interpretation and applicability of the analysis results.

With regards to cloud computing, the IT team observes that none of its systems are currently hosted in the cloud and that the team does not possess cloud-related skillsets. These facts alongside data privacy concerns lead the IT team to the decision to build an on-premise Big Data solution. The group notes that they will leave the option of cloud-based hosting open because there is some speculation that their internal CRM system may be replaced with a cloud-hosted, software-as-a-service CRM solution in the future.

Big Data Analytics Lifecycle

ETI's Big Data journey has reached the stage where its IT team possesses the necessary skills and the management is convinced of the potential benefits that a Big Data solution can bring in support of the business goals. The CEO and the directors are eager to see Big Data in action. In response to this, the IT team, in partnership with the business personnel, take on ETI's first Big Data project. After a thorough evaluation process, the "detection of fraudulent claims" objective is chosen as the first Big Data solution. The team then follows a step-by-step approach as set forth by the Big Data Analytics Lifecycle in pursuit of achieving this objective.

Business Case Evaluation

Carrying out Big Data analysis for the "detection of fraudulent claims" directly corresponds to a decrease in monetary loss and hence carries complete business backing. Although fraud occurs across all the four business sectors of ETI, in the interest of keeping the analysis somewhat straightforward, the scope of Big Data analysis is limited to identification of fraud in the building sector.

ETI provides building and contents insurance to both domestic and commercial customers. Although insurance fraud can both be opportunistic and organized, opportunistic fraud in the form of lying and exaggeration covers the majority of the cases. To measure the success of the Big Data solution for fraud detection, one of the KPIs set is the *reduction in fraudulent claims by 15%*.

Taking their budget into account, the team decides that their largest expense will be in the procuring of new infrastructure that is appropriate for building a Big Data solution environment. They realize that they will be leveraging open source technologies to support batch processing and therefore do not believe that a large, initial up-front investment is required for tooling. However, when they consider the broader Big Data analytics lifecycle, the team members realize that they should budget for the acquisition of additional data quality and cleansing tools and newer data visualization technologies. After accounting for these expenses, a cost-benefit analysis reveals that the investment in the Big Data solution can return itself several times over if the targeted fraud-detecting KPIs can be attained. As a result of this analysis, the team believes that a strong business case exists for using Big Data for enhanced data analysis.

Data Identification

A number of *internal* and *external* datasets are identified. Internal data includes policy data, insurance application documents, claim data, claim adjuster notes, incident photographs, call center agent notes and emails. External data includes social media data (Twitter feeds), weather reports, geographical (GIS) data and census data. Nearly all datasets go back five years in time. The claim data consists of historical claim data consisting of multiple fields where one of the fields specifies if the claim was *fraudulent* or *legitimate*.

Data Acquisition and Filtering

The policy data is obtained from the policy administration system, the claim data, incident photographs and claim adjuster notes are acquired from the claims management system and the insurance application documents are obtained from the document management system. The claim adjuster notes are currently embedded within the claim data. Hence a separate process is used to extract them. Call center agent notes and emails are obtained from the CRM system.

The rest of the datasets are acquired from third-party data providers. A compressed copy of the original version of all of the datasets is stored on-disk. From a provenance perspective, the following metadata is tracked to capture the pedigree of each dataset: dataset's name, source, size, format, checksum, acquired date and number of records. A quick check of the data qualities of Twitter feeds and weather reports suggests that around four to five percent of their records are corrupt. Consequently, two batch data filtering jobs are established to remove the corrupt records.

Data Extraction

The IT team observes that some of the datasets will need to be pre-processed in order to extract the required fields. For example, the tweets dataset is in JSON format. In order to be able to analyze the tweets, the *user id, timestamp* and the tweet *text* need to be extracted and converted to tabular form. Further, the weather dataset arrives in a hierarchical format (XML), and fields such as *timestamp, temperature forecast, wind speed forecast, wind direction forecast, snow forecast* and *flood forecast* are also extracted and saved in a tabular form.

Data Validation and Cleansing

To keep costs down, ETI is currently using free versions of the weather and the census datasets that are not guaranteed to be 100% accurate. As a result, these datasets need to be validated and cleansed. Based on the published field information, the team is able to check the extracted fields for typographical errors and any incorrect data as well as data type and range validation. A rule is established that a record will not be removed if it contains some meaningful level of information even though some of its fields may contain invalid data.

Data Aggregation and Representation

For meaningful analysis of data, it is decided to join together policy data, claim data and call center agent notes in a single dataset that is tabular in nature where each field can be referenced via a data query. It is thought that this will not only help with the current data analysis task of detecting fraudulent claims but will also help with other data analysis tasks, such as risk evaluation and speedy settlement of claims. The resulting dataset is stored in a NoSQL database.

Data Analysis

The IT team involves the data analysts at this stage as it does not have the right skillset for analyzing data in support of detecting fraudulent claims. In order to be able to detect fraudulent transactions, first the nature of fraudulent claims needs to be analyzed in order to find which characteristics differentiate a fraudulent claim from a legitimate claim. For this, the *exploratory data analysis* approach is taken. As part of this analysis, a range of analysis techniques are applied, some of which are discussed in Chapter 8. This stage is repeated a number of times as the results generated after the first pass are not conclusive enough to comprehend what makes a fraudulent claim different from a legitimate claim. As part of this exercise, attributes that are less indicative of a fraudulent claim are dropped while attributes that carry a direct relationship are kept or added.

Data Visualization

The team has discovered some interesting findings and now needs to convey the results to the actuaries, underwriters and claim adjusters. Different visualization methods are used including bar and line graphs and scatter plots. Scatter plots are used to analyze groups of fraudulent and legitimate claims in the light of different factors, such as *customer age, age of policy, number of claims made* and *value of claim.*

Utilization of Analysis Results

Based on the data analysis results, the underwriting and the claims settlement users have now developed an understanding of the nature of fraudulent claims. However, in order to realize tangible benefits from this data analysis exercise, a model based on a machine-learning technique is generated, which is then incorporated into the existing claim processing system to flag fraudulent claims. The involved machine learning technique will be discussed in Chapter 8.

Chapter 4

Enterprise Technologies and Big Data Business Intelligence

Online Transaction Processing (OLTP)

Online Analytical Processing (OLAP)

Extract Transform Load (ETL)

Data Warehouses

Data Marts

Traditional BI

Big Data BI

As described in Chapter 2, in an enterprise executed as a layered system, the strategic layer constrains the tactical layer, which directs the operational layer. The alignment of layers is captured through metrics and performance indicators, which provide the operational layer with insight into how its processes are executing. These measurements are aggregated and enhanced with additional meaning to become KPIs, through which managers of the tactical layer can assess corporate performance, or business execution. The KPIs are related with other measurements and understandings that are used to assess critical success factors. Ultimately, this series of enrichment corresponds with the transformation of data into information, information into knowledge and knowledge into wisdom.

This chapter discusses the enterprise technologies that support this transformation. Data is held within the operational-level information systems of an organization. Moreover, database structure is leveraged with queries to generate information. Higher up the analytic food chain are analytical processing systems. These systems leverage multi-dimensional structures to answer more complex queries and provide deeper insight into business operations. On a larger scale, data is collected from throughout the enterprise and warehoused in a data warehouse. It is from these data stores that management gains insight into broader corporate performance and KPIs.

This chapter covers the following topics:

- Online Transaction Processing (OLTP)
- Online Analytical Processing (OLAP)
- Extract Transform Load (ETL)
- Data Warehouses
- Data Marts
- Traditional BI
- Big Data BI

Online Transaction Processing (OLTP)

OLTP is a software system that processes transaction-oriented data. The term "online transaction" refers to the completion of an activity in realtime and is not batch-processed. OLTP systems store operational data that is normalized. This data is a common source of structured data and serves as input to many analytic processes. Big Data analysis results can be used to augment OLTP data stored in the underlying relational databases. OLTP systems, for example a point of sale system, execute business processes in support of corporate operations. As shown in Figure 4.1, they perform transactions against a relational database.

The queries supported by OLTP systems are comprised of simple insert, delete and update operations with sub-second response times. Examples include ticket reservation systems, banking and point of sale systems.

Figure 4.1
OLTP systems perform
simple database operations
to provide sub-second
response times.

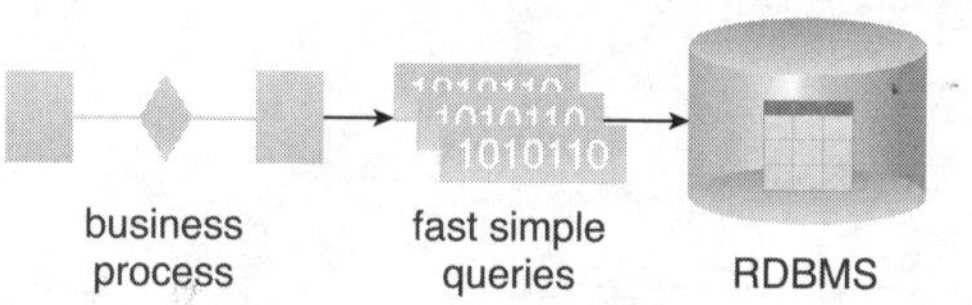

business process   fast simple queries   RDBMS

Online Analytical Processing (OLAP)

Online analytical processing (OLAP) systems are used for processing data analysis queries. OLAPs form an integral part of business intelligence, data mining and machine learning processes. They are relevant to Big Data in that they can serve as both a data source as well as a data sink that is capable of receiving data. They are used in diagnostic, predictive and prescriptive analytics. As shown in Figure 4.2, OLAP systems perform long-running, complex queries against a multidimensional database whose structure is optimized for performing advanced analytics.

OLAP systems store historical data that is aggregated and denormalized to support fast reporting capability. They further use databases that store historical data in multidimensional structures and can answer complex queries based on the relationships between multiple aspects of the data.

Figure 4.2
OLAP systems use
multidimensional
databases.

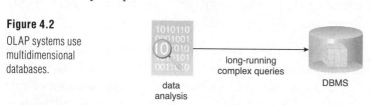

data analysis   long-running complex queries   DBMS

Extract Transform Load (ETL)

Extract Transform Load (ETL) is a process of loading data from a source system into a target system. The source system can be a database, a flat file, or an application. Similarly, the target system can be a database or some other storage system.

ETL represents the main operation through which data warehouses are fed data. A Big Data solution encompasses the ETL feature-set for converting data of different types. Figure 4.3 shows that the required data is first obtained or extracted from the sources, after which the extracts are modified or transformed by the application of rules. Finally, the data is inserted or loaded into the target system.

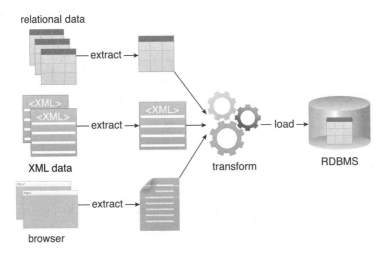

Figure 4.3
An ETL process can extract data from multiple sources and transform it for loading into a single target system.

Data Warehouses

A data warehouse is a central, enterprise-wide repository consisting of historical and current data. Data warehouses are heavily used by BI to run various analytical queries, and they usually interface with an OLAP system to support multi-dimensional analytical queries, as shown in Figure 4.4.

Data pertaining to multiple business entities from different operational systems is periodically extracted, validated, transformed and consolidated into a single denormalized database. With periodic data imports from across the enterprise, the amount of data contained in a given data warehouse will continue to increase. Over time this leads to slower query response times for data analysis tasks. To resolve this shortcoming, data warehouses usually contain optimized databases, called analytical databases, to handle reporting and data analysis tasks. An analytical database can exist as a separate DBMS, as in the case of an OLAP database.

Figure 4.4

Batch jobs periodically load data into a data warehouse from operational systems like ERP, CRM and SCM.

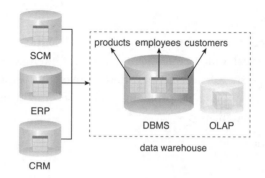

Data Marts

A data mart is a subset of the data stored in a data warehouse that typically belongs to a department, division, or specific line of business. Data warehouses can have multiple data marts. As shown in Figure 4.5, enterprise-wide data is collected and business entities are then extracted. Domain-specific entities are persisted into the data warehouse via an ETL process.

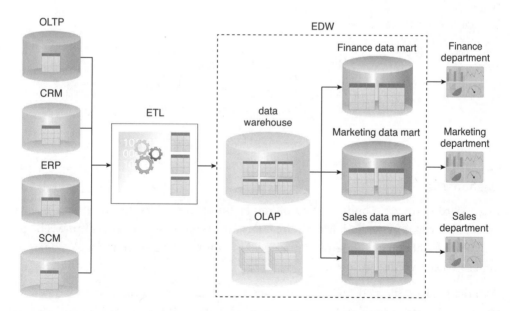

Figure 4.5

A data warehouse's single version of "truth" is based on cleansed data, which is a prerequisite for accurate and error-free reports, as per the output shown on the right.

Traditional BI

Traditional BI primarily utilizes descriptive and diagnostic analytics to provide information on historical and current events. It is not "intelligent" because it only provides answers to correctly formulated questions. Correctly formulating questions requires an understanding of business problems and issues and of the data itself. BI reports on different KPIs through:

- ad-hoc reports

- dashboards

Ad-hoc Reports

Ad-hoc reporting is a process that involves manually processing data to produce custom-made reports, as shown in Figure 4.6. The focus of an ad-hoc report is usually on a specific area of the business, such as its marketing or supply chain management. The generated custom reports are detailed and often tabular in nature.

Figure 4.6
OLAP and OLTP data sources can be used by BI tools for both ad-hoc reporting and dashboards.

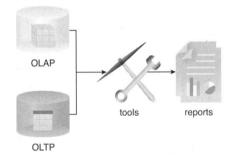

Dashboards

Dashboards provide a holistic view of key business areas. The information displayed on dashboards is generated at periodic intervals in realtime or near-realtime. The presentation of data on dashboards is graphical in nature, using bar charts, pie charts and gauges, as shown in Figure 4.7.

As previously explained, data warehouses and data marts contain consolidated and validated information about enterprise-wide business entities. Traditional BI cannot function effectively without data marts because they contain the optimized and segregated data that BI requires for reporting purposes. Without data marts, data needs to be extracted from the data warehouse via an ETL process on an ad-hoc basis whenever a query needs to be run. This increases the time and effort to execute queries and generate reports.

Figure 4.7
BI tools use both OLAP and OLTP to display the information on dashboards.

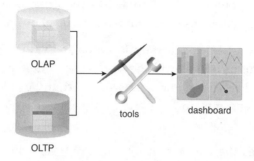

Traditional BI uses data warehouses and data marts for reporting and data analysis because they allow complex data analysis queries with multiple joins and aggregations to be issued, as shown in Figure 4.8.

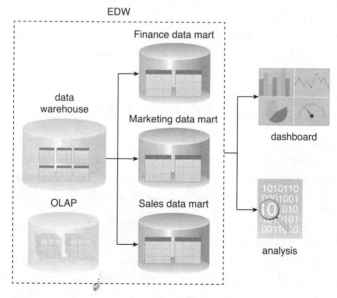

Figure 4.8
An example of traditional BI.

Big Data BI

Big Data BI builds upon traditional BI by acting on the cleansed, consolidated enterprise-wide data in the data warehouse and combining it with semi-structured and unstructured data sources. It comprises both predictive and prescriptive analytics to facilitate the development of an enterprise-wide understanding of business performance.

While traditional BI analyses generally focus on individual business processes, Big Data BI analyses focus on multiple business processes simultaneously. This helps reveal patterns and anomalies across a broader scope within the enterprise. It also leads to data discovery by identifying insights and information that may have been previously absent or unknown.

Big Data BI requires the analysis of unstructured, semi-structured and structured data residing in the enterprise data warehouse. This requires a "next-generation" data warehouse that uses new features and technologies to store cleansed data originating from a variety of sources in a single uniform data format. The coupling of a traditional data warehouse with these new technologies results in a hybrid data warehouse. This warehouse acts as a uniform and central repository of structured, semi-structured and unstructured data that can provide Big Data BI tools with all of the required data. This eliminates the need for Big Data BI tools to have to connect to multiple data sources to retrieve or access data. In Figure 4.9, a next-generation data warehouse establishes a standardized data access layer across a range of data sources.

Traditional Data Visualization

Data visualization is a technique whereby analytical results are graphically communicated using elements like charts, maps, data grids, infographics and alerts. Graphically representing data can make it easier to understand reports, view trends and identify patterns.

Traditional data visualization provides mostly static charts and graphs in reports and dashboards, whereas contemporary data visualization tools are interactive and can provide both summarized and detailed views of data. They are designed to help people who lack statistical and/or mathematical skills to better understand analytical results without having to resort to spreadsheets.

Traditional data visualization tools query data from relational databases, OLAP systems, data warehouses and spreadsheets to present both descriptive and diagnostic analytics results.

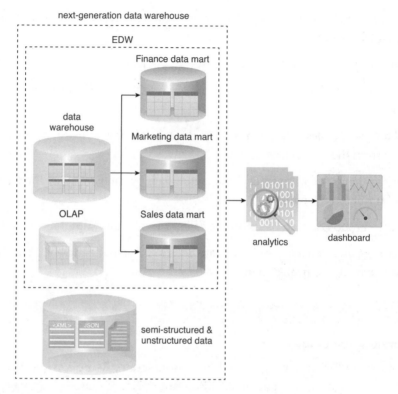

Figure 4.9
A next-generation data warehouse.

Data Visualization for Big Data

Big Data solutions require data visualization tools that can seamlessly connect to structured, semi-structured and unstructured data sources and are further capable of handling millions of data records. Data visualization tools for Big Data solutions generally use in-memory analytical technologies that reduce the latency normally attributed to traditional, disk-based data visualization tools.

Advanced data visualization tools for Big Data solutions incorporate predictive and prescriptive data analytics and data transformation features. These tools eliminate the need for data pre-processing methods, such as ETL. The tools also provide the ability to directly connect to structured, semi-structured and unstructured data sources. As part of Big Data solutions, advanced data visualization tools can join structured and unstructured data that is kept in memory for fast data access. Queries and statistical formulas can then be applied as part of various data analysis tasks for viewing data in a user-friendly format, such as on a dashboard.

Common features of visualization tools used in Big Data:

- *Aggregation* – provides a holistic and summarized view of data across multiple contexts

- *Drill-down* – enables a detailed view of the data of interest by focusing in on a data subset from the summarized view

- *Filtering* – helps focus on a particular set of data by filtering away the data that is not of immediate interest

- *Roll-up* – groups data across multiple categories to show subtotals and totals

- *What-if analysis* – enables multiple outcomes to be visualized by enabling related factors to be dynamically changed.

CASE STUDY EXAMPLE

Enterprise Technology

ETI employs OLTP in almost every business function. Its policy quotation, policy administration, claims management, billing, enterprise resource planning (ERP) and customer relationship management (CRM) systems are all OLTP-based. An example of ETI's employment of OLTP occurs whenever there is the submission of a new claim, for it results in the creation of a new record in the *claim* table found within the relational database used by the claims management system. Similarly, as the claim gets processed by the claim adjuster, its status changes from *submitted* to *assigned* and from *assigned* to *processing* and finally to *processed* through simple database update operations.

The EDW is populated weekly via multiple ETL operations that involve extracting data from tables in the relational databases used by operational systems, validating and transforming the data and loading it into the EDW's database. Data extracted from the operational systems is in a flat file format that is first imported into a staging database, where it is transformed by the execution of various scripts. One ETL process that deals with customer data involves the application of several data validation rules, one of which is to confirm that each customer has both the *first* and *surname* fields populated with meaningful characters. Also, as part of the same ETL process, the first two lines of the *address* are joined together.

The EDW includes an OLAP system where data is kept in the form of cubes that enable the execution of various reporting queries. For example, the *policy* cube is made up of calculations of *policies sold* (the *fact* table) and dimensions of *location*, *type* and *time* (*dimension* tables.) The analysts perform queries on different cubes as part of business intelligence (BI) activities. For security and fast query response, the EDW further contains two data marts. One of them is comprised of *claim* and *policy* data that is used by the actuaries and the legal team for various data analyses, including risk assessment and regulatory compliance assurance. The second one contains sales-related data that is used by the sales team to monitor sales and set future sales strategies.

Big Data Business Intelligence

As established, ETI currently employs BI that falls into the category of traditional BI. One particular dashboard used by the sales team displays various policy-related KPIs via different charts, such as a breakdown of sold policies by type, region and value and policies expiring each month. Different dashboards inform agents of their current performances, such as commissions earned and whether or not they are on track for achieving their monthly targets. Both of these dashboards are fed data from the sales data mart.

In the call center, a scoreboard provides vital statistics related to daily operations of the center, such as the number of calls in queue, average waiting time, number of calls dropped and calls by type. This scoreboard is fed data directly from the CRM's relational database with a BI product that provides a simple user interface for constructing different SQL queries that are periodically executed to obtain required KPIs. The legal team and the actuaries, however, generate some ad-hoc reports that resemble a spreadsheet. Some of these reports are sent to the regulatory authorities as part of assuring continuous regulatory compliance.

ETI believes that the adoption of Big Data BI will greatly help in achieving its strategic goals. For example, the incorporation of social media along with a call center agent's notes may provide a better understanding of the reasons behind a customer's defection. Similarly, the legitimacy of a filed claim can be ascertained more quickly if valuable information can be harvested from the documents submitted at the time a policy was purchased and cross-referenced against the claim data. This information can then be correlated with similar claims to detect fraud.

With regards to data visualization, the BI tools used by the analysts currently only operate on structured data. In terms of sophistication and ease of use, most of these tools provide point-and-click functionality where either a wizard can be used or the required fields can be selected manually from the relevant tables displayed graphically to construct a database query. The query results can then be displayed by choosing the relevant charts and graphs. The end result is a dashboard where different statistics are displayed. The dashboard can be configured to add filtering, aggregation and drill-down options. An example of this could be a user who clicks on a quarterly sales figures chart and is taken to a monthly breakdown of sales figures. Although a dashboard that provides the what-if analysis feature is not currently supported, having one would allow the actuaries to quickly ascertain different risk levels by changing relevant risk factors.

Part II

Storing and Analyzing Big Data

As presented in Part I, the drivers behind Big Data adoption are both business- and technology-related. In the remainder of this book, the focus shifts from providing a high-level understanding of Big Data and its business implications to covering key concepts related to the two main Big Data concerns: storage and analysis.

Part II has the following structure:

- Chapter 5 explores key concepts related to the storage of Big Data datasets. These concepts inform the reader of how Big Data storage has radically different characteristics than the relational database technology common to traditional business information systems.

- Chapter 6 provides insights into how Big Data datasets are processed by leveraging distributed and parallel processing capabilities. This is further illustrated with an examination of the MapReduce framework, which shows how it leverages a divide-and-conquer approach to efficiently process Big Data datasets.

- Chapter 7 expands upon the storage topic, showing how the concepts from Chapter 5 are implemented with different flavors of NoSQL database technology. The requirements of batch and realtime processing modes are further explored from the perspective of on-disk and in-memory storage options.

- Chapter 8 provides an introduction to a range of Big Data analysis techniques. The analysis of Big Data leverages statistical approaches for quantitative and qualitative analysis, whereas computational approaches are used for data mining and machine learning.

The technology concepts covered in Part II are important for business and technology leaders as well as decision-makers who will be called upon to evaluate the business case for Big Data adoption in their enterprises.

Chapter 5

Big Data Storage Concepts

D ata acquired from external sources is often not in a format or structure that can be directly processed. To overcome these incompatibilities and prepare data for storage and processing, data wrangling is necessary. Data wrangling includes steps to filter, cleanse and otherwise prepare the data for downstream analysis. From a storage perspective, a copy of the data is first stored in its acquired format, and, after wrangling, the prepared data needs to be stored again. Typically, storage is required whenever the following occurs:

- external datasets are acquired, or internal data will be used in a Big Data environment

- data is manipulated to be made amenable for data analysis

- data is processed via an ETL activity, or output is generated as a result of an analytical operation

Due to the need to store Big Data datasets, often in multiple copies, innovative storage strategies and technologies have been created to achieve cost-effective and highly scalable storage solutions. In order to understand the underlying mechanisms behind Big Data storage technology, the following topics are introduced in this chapter:

- clusters

- file systems and distributed files systems

- NoSQL

- sharding

- replication

- CAP theorem

- ACID

- BASE

Clusters

In computing, a cluster is a tightly coupled collection of servers, or nodes. These servers usually have the same hardware specifications and are connected together via a network to work as a single unit, as shown in Figure 5.1. Each node in the cluster has its own dedicated resources, such as memory, a processor, and a hard drive. A cluster can execute a task by splitting it into small pieces and distributing their execution onto different computers that belong to the cluster.

Figure 5.1
The symbol used to represent a cluster.

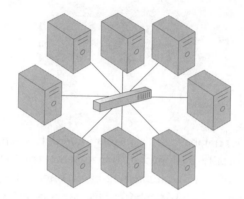

File Systems and Distributed File Systems

A file system is the method of storing and organizing data on a storage device, such as flash drives, DVDs and hard drives. A file is an atomic unit of storage used by the file system to store data. A file system provides a logical view of the data stored on the storage device and presents it as a tree structure of directories and files as pictured in Figure 5.2. Operating systems employ file systems to store and retrieve data on behalf of applications. Each operating system provides support for one or more file systems, for example NTFS on Microsoft Windows and ext on Linux.

Figure 5.2
The symbol used to represent a file system.

A distributed file system is a file system that can store large files spread across the nodes of a cluster, as illustrated in Figure 5.3. To the client, files appear to be local; however, this is only a logical view as physically the files are distributed throughout the cluster. This local view is presented via the distributed file system and it enables the files to be accessed from multiple locations. Examples include the Google File System (GFS) and Hadoop Distributed File System (HDFS).

Figure 5.3

The symbol used to
represent distributed
file systems.

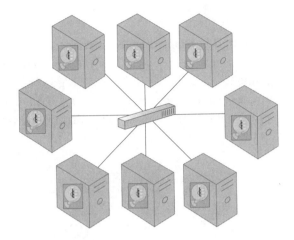

NoSQL

A Not-only SQL (NoSQL) database is a non-relational database that is highly scalable,
fault-tolerant and specifically designed to house semi-structured and unstructured
data. A NoSQL database often provides an API-based query interface that can be called
from within an application. NoSQL databases also support query languages other than
Structured Query Language (SQL) because SQL was designed to query structured data
stored within a relational database. As an example, a NoSQL database that is optimized
to store XML files will often use XQuery as the query language. Likewise, a NoSQL
database designed to store RDF data will use SPARQL to query the relationships it contains. That being said, there are some NoSQL databases that also provide an SQL-like
query interface, as shown in Figure 5.4.

Figure 5.4

A NoSQL database can
provide an API- or SQL-like
query interface.

Sharding

Sharding is the process of horizontally partitioning a large dataset into a collection of smaller, more manageable datasets called *shards*. The shards are distributed across multiple nodes, where a node is a server or a machine (Figure 5.5). Each shard is stored on a separate node and each node is responsible for only the data stored on it. Each shard shares the same schema, and all shards collectively represent the complete dataset.

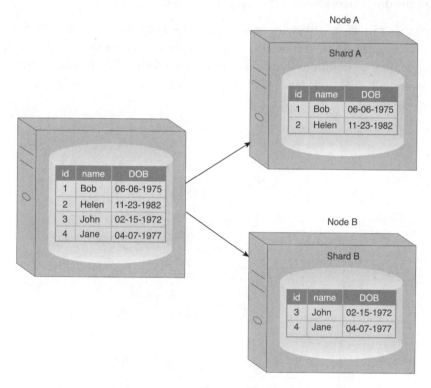

Figure 5.5

An example of sharding where a dataset is spread across Node A and Node B, resulting in Shard A and Shard B, respectively.

Sharding is often transparent to the client, but this is not a requirement. Sharding allows the distribution of processing loads across multiple nodes to achieve horizontal scalability. Horizontal scaling is a method for increasing a system's capacity by adding similar or higher capacity resources alongside existing resources. Since each node is responsible for only a part of the whole dataset, read/write times are greatly improved.

Figure 5.6 presents an illustration of how sharding works in practice:

1. Each shard can independently service reads and writes for the specific subset of data that it is responsible for.

2. Depending on the query, data may need to be fetched from both shards.

A benefit of sharding is that it provides partial tolerance toward failures. In case of a node failure, only data stored on that node is affected.

With regards to data partitioning, query patterns need to be taken into account so that shards themselves do not become performance bottlenecks. For example, queries requiring data from multiple shards will impose performance penalties. Data locality keeps commonly accessed data co-located on a single shard and helps counter such performance issues.

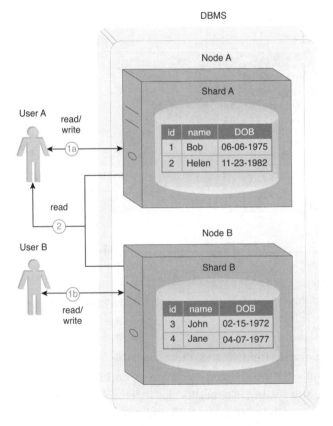

Figure 5.6

A sharding example where data is fetched from both Node A and Node B.

Replication

Replication stores multiple copies of a dataset, known as *replicas*, on multiple nodes (Figure 5.7). Replication provides scalability and availability due to the fact that the same data is replicated on various nodes. Fault tolerance is also achieved since data redundancy ensures that data is not lost when an individual node fails. There are two different methods that are used to implement replication:

- master-slave
- peer-to-peer

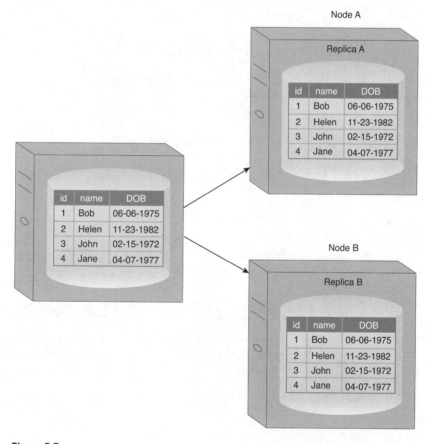

Figure 5.7

An example of replication where a dataset is replicated to Node A and Node B, resulting in Replica A and Replica B.

Master-Slave

During master-slave replication, nodes are arranged in a master-slave configuration, and all data is written to a master node. Once saved, the data is replicated over to multiple slave nodes. All external write requests, including insert, update and delete, occur on the master node, whereas read requests can be fulfilled by any slave node. In Figure 5.8, writes are managed by the master node and data can be read from either Slave A or Slave B.

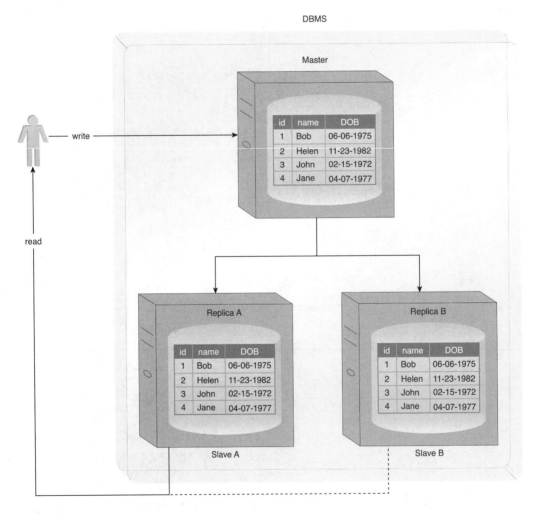

Figure 5.8

An example of master-slave replication where Master A is the single point of contact for all writes, and data can be read from Slave A and Slave B.

Master-slave replication is ideal for read intensive loads rather than write intensive loads since growing read demands can be managed by horizontal scaling to add more slave nodes. Writes are consistent, as all writes are coordinated by the master node. The implication is that write performance will suffer as the amount of writes increases. If the master node fails, reads are still possible via any of the slave nodes.

A slave node can be configured as a backup node for the master node. In the event that the master node fails, writes are not supported until a master node is reestablished. The master node is either resurrected from a backup of the master node, or a new master node is chosen from the slave nodes.

One concern with master-slave replication is read inconsistency, which can be an issue if a slave node is read prior to an update to the master being copied to it. To ensure read consistency, a voting system can be implemented where a read is declared consistent if the majority of the slaves contain the same version of the record. Implementation of such a voting system requires a reliable and fast communication mechanism between the slaves.

Figure 5.9 illustrates a scenario where read inconsistency occurs.

1. User A updates data.

2. The data is copied over to Slave A by the Master.

3. Before the data is copied over to Slave B, User B tries to read the data from Slave B, which results in an inconsistent read.

4. The data will eventually become consistent when Slave B is updated by the Master.

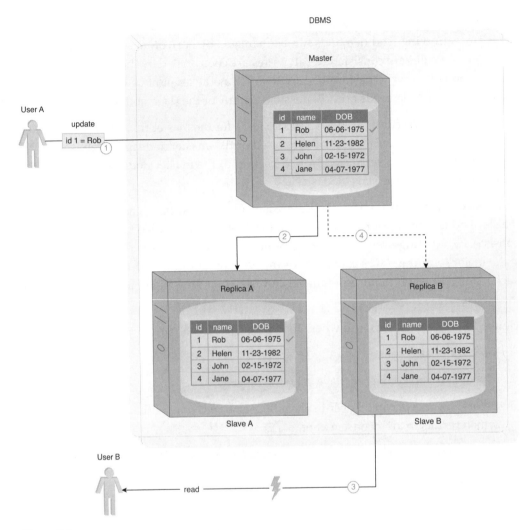

Figure 5.9

An example of master-slave replication where read inconsistency occurs.

Peer-to-Peer

With peer-to-peer replication, all nodes operate at the same level. In other words, there is not a master-slave relationship between the nodes. Each node, known as a peer, is equally capable of handling reads and writes. Each write is copied to all peers, as illustrated in Figure 5.10.

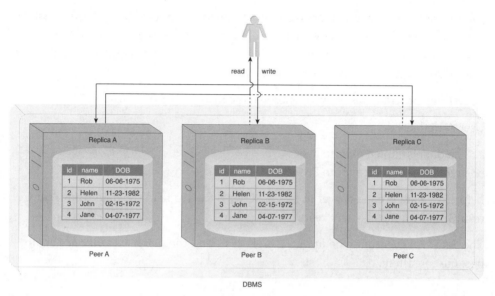

Figure 5.10
Writes are copied to Peers A, B and C simultaneously. Data is read from Peer A, but it can also be read from Peers B or C.

Peer-to-peer replication is prone to write inconsistencies that occur as a result of a simultaneous update of the same data across multiple peers. This can be addressed by implementing either a pessimistic or optimistic concurrency strategy.

- Pessimistic concurrency is a proactive strategy that prevents inconsistency. It uses locking to ensure that only one update to a record can occur at a time. However, this is detrimental to availability since the database record being updated remains unavailable until all locks are released.

- Optimistic concurrency is a reactive strategy that does not use locking. Instead, it allows inconsistency to occur with knowledge that eventually consistency will be achieved after all updates have propagated.

With optimistic concurrency, peers may remain inconsistent for some period of time before attaining consistency. However, the database remains available as no locking is involved. Like master-slave replication, reads can be inconsistent during the time period when some of the peers have completed their updates while others perform their updates. However, reads eventually become consistent when the updates have been executed on all peers.

To ensure read consistency, a voting system can be implemented where a read is declared consistent if the majority of the peers contain the same version of the record. As previously indicated, implementation of such a voting system requires a reliable and fast communication mechanism between the peers.

Figure 5.11 demonstrates a scenario where an inconsistent read occurs.

1. User A updates data.

2. a. The data is copied over to Peer A.
    b. The data is copied over to Peer B.

3. Before the data is copied over to Peer C, User B tries to read the data from Peer C, resulting in an inconsistent read.

4. The data will eventually be updated on Peer C, and the database will once again become consistent.

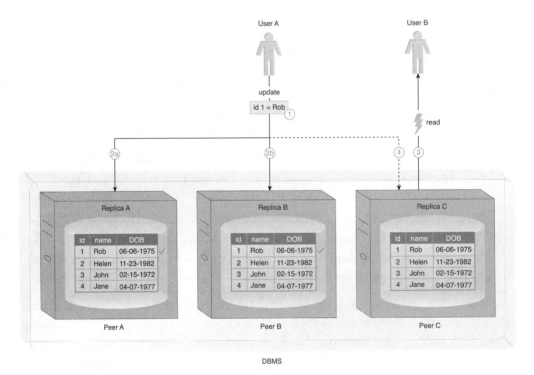

Figure 5.11
An example of peer-to-peer replication where an inconsistent read occurs.

Sharding and Replication

To improve on the limited fault tolerance offered by sharding, while additionally benefiting from the increased availability and scalability of replication, both sharding and replication can be combined, as shown in Figure 5.12.

This section covers the following combinations:

- sharding and master-slave replication
- sharding and peer-to-peer replication

Figure 5.12

A comparison of sharding and replication that shows how a dataset is distributed between two nodes with the different approaches.

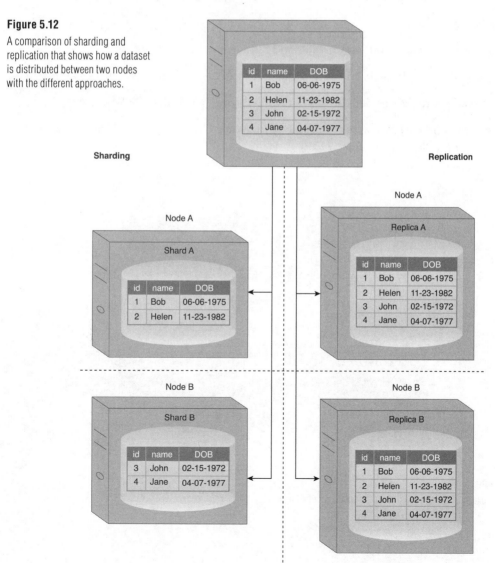

Combining Sharding and Master-Slave Replication

When sharding is combined with master-slave replication, multiple shards become slaves of a single master, and the master itself is a shard. Although this results in multiple masters, a single slave-shard can only be managed by a single master-shard.

Write consistency is maintained by the master-shard. However, if the master-shard becomes non-operational or a network outage occurs, fault tolerance with regards to write operations is impacted. Replicas of shards are kept on multiple slave nodes to provide scalability and fault tolerance for read operations.

In Figure 5.13:

- Each node acts both as a master and a slave for different shards.

- Writes (id = 2) to Shard A are regulated by Node A, as it is the master for Shard A.

- Node A replicates data (id = 2) to Node B, which is a slave for Shard A.

- Reads (id = 4) can be served directly by either Node B or Node C as they each contain Shard B.

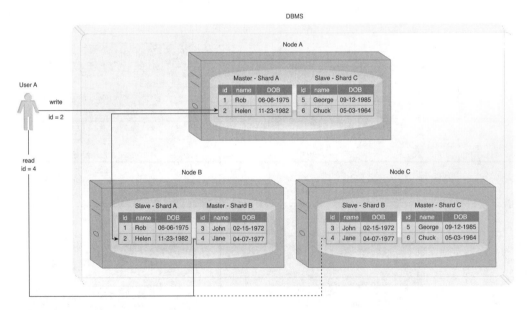

Figure 5.13

An example that shows the combination of sharding and master-slave replication.

Combining Sharding and Peer-to-Peer Replication

When combining sharding with peer-to-peer replication, each shard is replicated to multiple peers, and each peer is only responsible for a subset of the overall dataset. Collectively, this helps achieve increased scalability and fault tolerance. As there is no master involved, there is no single point of failure and fault-tolerance for both read and write operations is supported.

In Figure 5.14:

- Each node contains replicas of two different shards.

- Writes (id = 3) are replicated to both Node A and Node C (Peers) as they are responsible for Shard C.

- Reads (id = 6) can be served by either Node B or Node C as they each contain Shard B.

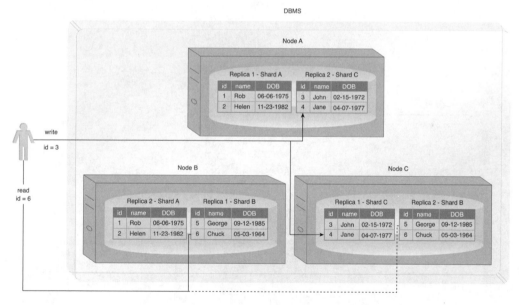

Figure 5.14
An example of the combination of sharding and peer-to-peer replication.

CAP Theorem

The Consistency, Availability, and Partition tolerance (CAP) theorem, also known as Brewer's theorem, expresses a triple constraint related to distributed database systems. It states that a distributed database system, running on a cluster, can only provide two of the following three properties:

- *Consistency* – A read from any node results in the same data across multiple nodes (Figure 5.15).

- *Availability* – A read/write request will always be acknowledged in the form of a success or a failure (Figure 5.16).

- *Partition tolerance* – The database system can tolerate communication outages that split the cluster into multiple silos and can still service read/write requests (Figure 5.16).

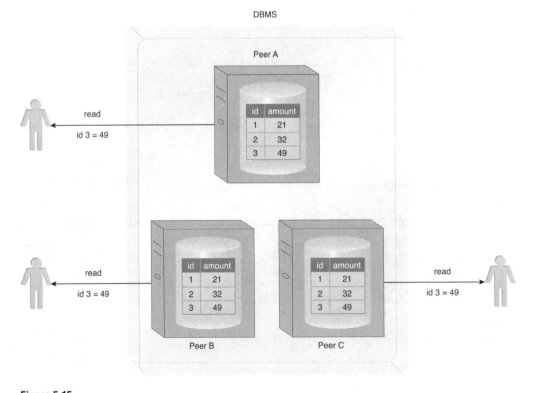

Figure 5.15

Consistency: all three users get the same value for the amount column even though three different nodes are serving the record.

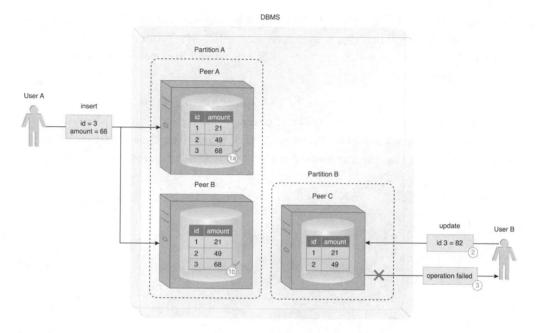

Figure 5.16

Availability and partition tolerance: in the event of a communication failure, requests from both users are still serviced (1, 2). However, with User B, the update fails as the record with id = 3 has not been copied over to Peer C. The user is duly notified (3) that the update has failed.

The following scenarios demonstrate why only two of the three properties of the CAP theorem are simultaneously supportable. To aid this discussion, Figure 5.17 provides a Venn diagram showing the areas of overlap between consistency, availability and partition tolerance.

If consistency (C) and availability (A) are required, available nodes need to communicate to ensure consistency (C). Therefore, partition tolerance (P) is not possible.

If consistency (C) and partition tolerance (P) are required, nodes cannot remain available (A) as the nodes will become unavailable while achieving a state of consistency (C).

If availability (A) and partition tolerance (P) are required, then consistency (C) is not possible because of the data communication requirement between the nodes. So, the database can remain available (A) but with inconsistent results.

In a distributed database, scalability and fault tolerance can be improved through additional nodes, although this challenges consistency (C). The addition of nodes can also cause availability (A) to suffer due to the latency caused by increased communication between nodes.

Distributed database systems cannot be 100% partition tolerant (P). Although communication outages are rare and temporary, partition tolerance (P) must always be supported by a distributed database; therefore, CAP is generally a choice between choosing either C+P or A+P. The requirements of the system will dictate which is chosen.

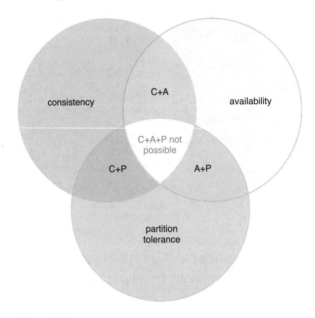

Figure 5.17
A Venn diagram summarizing the CAP theorem.

ACID

ACID is a database design principle related to transaction management. It is an acronym that stands for:

- atomicity
- consistency
- isolation
- durability

ACID is a transaction management style that leverages pessimistic concurrency controls to ensure consistency is maintained through the application of record locks. ACID is the traditional approach to database transaction management as it is leveraged by relational database management systems.

Atomicity ensures that all operations will always succeed or fail completely. In other words, there are no partial transactions.

The following steps are illustrated in Figure 5.18:

1. A user attempts to update three records as a part of a transaction.

2. Two records are successfully updated before the occurrence of an error.

3. As a result, the database roll backs any partial effects of the transaction and puts the system back to its prior state.

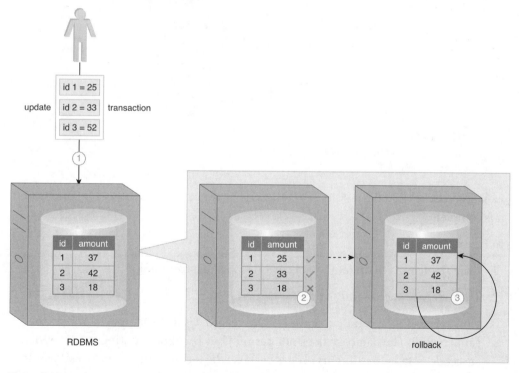

Figure 5.18

An example of the atomicity property of ACID is evident here.

Consistency ensures that the database will always remain in a consistent state by ensuring that only data that conforms to the constraints of the database schema can be written to the database. Thus a database that is in a consistent state will remain in a consistent state following a successful transaction.

In Figure 5.19:

1. A user attempts to update the amount column of the table that is of type float with a varchar value.

2. The database applies its validation check and rejects this update because the value violates the constraint checks for the amount column.

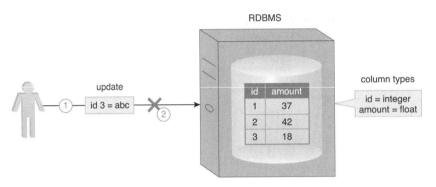

Figure 5.19
An example of the consistency of ACID.

Isolation ensures that the results of a transaction are not visible to other operations until it is complete.

In Figure 5.20:

1. User A attempts to update two records as part of a transaction.

2. The database successfully updates the first record.

3. However, before it can update the second record, User B attempts to update the same record. The database does not permit User B's update until User A's update succeeds or fails in full. This occurs because the record with id3 is locked by the database until the transaction is complete.

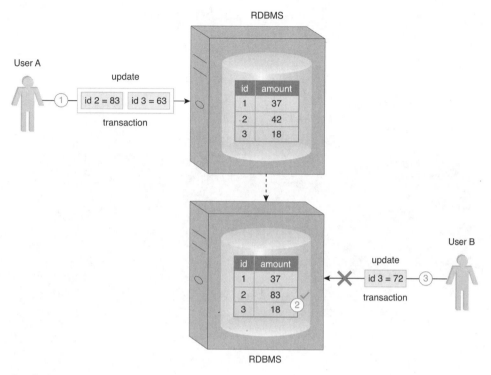

Figure 5.20
An example of the isolation property of ACID.

Durability ensures that the results of an operation are permanent. In other words, once a transaction has been committed, it cannot be rolled back. This is irrespective of any system failure.

In Figure 5.21:

1. A user updates a record as part of a transaction.

2. The database successfully updates the record.

3. Right after this update, a power failure occurs. The database maintains its state while there is no power.

4. The power is resumed.

5. The database serves the record as per last update when requested by the user.

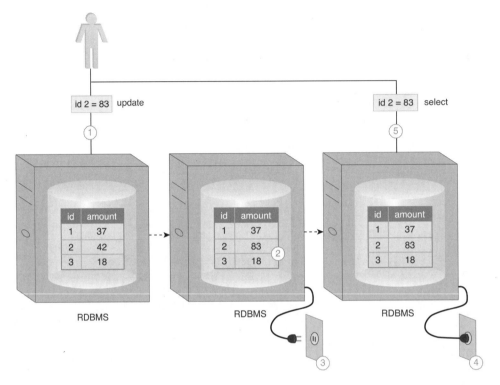

Figure 5.21
The durability characteristic of ACID.

Figure 5.22 shows the results of the application of the ACID principle:

1. User A attempts to update a record as part of a transaction.

2. The database validates the value and the update is successfully applied.

3. After the successful completion of the transaction, when Users B and C request the same record, the database provides the updated value to both the users.

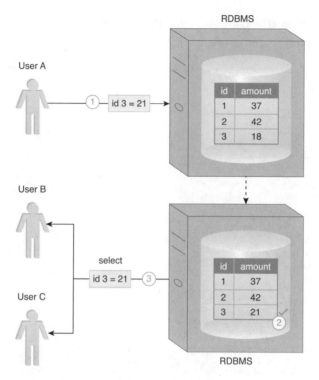

Figure 5.22
The ACID principle results in consistent database behavior.

BASE

BASE is a database design principle based on the CAP theorem and leveraged by database systems that use distributed technology. BASE stands for:

- basically available

- soft state

- eventual consistency

When a database supports BASE, it favors availability over consistency. In other words, the database is A+P from a CAP perspective. In essence, BASE leverages optimistic concurrency by relaxing the strong consistency constraints mandated by the ACID properties.

If a database is "basically available," that database will always acknowledge a client's request, either in the form of the requested data or a success/failure notification.

In Figure 5.23, the database is basically available, even though it has been partitioned as a result of a network failure.

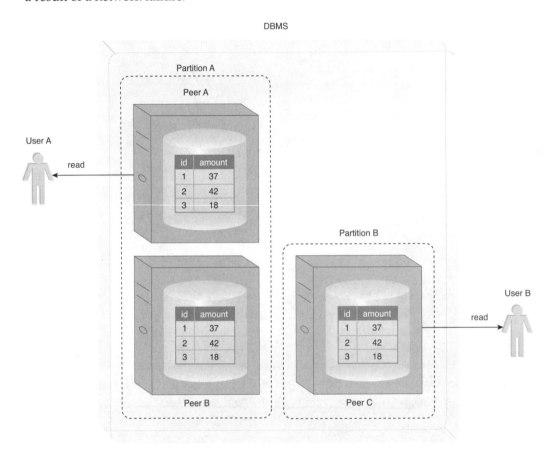

Figure 5.23
User A and User B receive data despite the database being partitioned by a network failure.

Soft state means that a database may be in an inconsistent state when data is read; thus, the results may change if the same data is requested again. This is because the data could be updated for consistency, even though no user has written to the database between the two reads. This property is closely related to eventual consistency.

In Figure 5.24:

1. User A updates a record on Peer A.

2. Before the other peers are updated, User B requests the same record from Peer C.

3. The database is now in a soft state, and stale data is returned to User B.

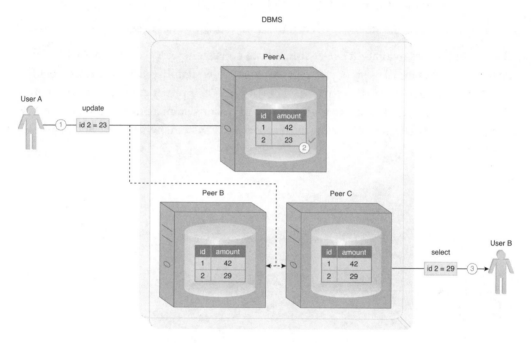

Figure 5.24
An example of the soft state property of BASE is shown here.

Eventual consistency is the state in which reads by different clients, immediately following a write to the database, may not return consistent results. The database only attains consistency once the changes have been propagated to all nodes. While the database is in the process of attaining the state of eventual consistency, it will be in a soft state.

In Figure 5.25:

1. User A updates a record.

2. The record only gets updated at Peer A, but before the other peers can be updated, User B requests the same record.

3. The database is now in a soft state. Stale data is returned to User B from Peer C.

4. However, the consistency is eventually attained, and User C gets the correct value.

BASE emphasizes availability over immediate consistency, in contrast to ACID, which ensures immediate consistency at the expense of availability due to record locking. This soft approach toward consistency allows BASE compliant databases to serve multiple clients without any latency albeit serving inconsistent results. However, BASE-compliant databases are not useful for transactional systems where lack of consistency is a concern.

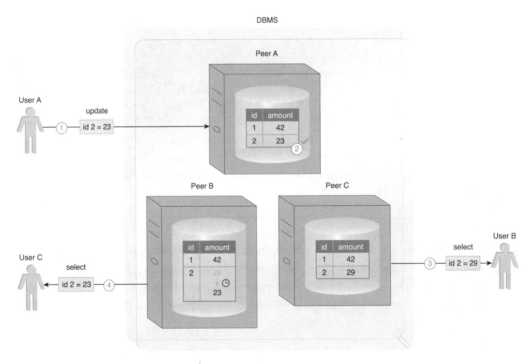

Figure 5.25

An example of the eventual consistency property of BASE.

ETI's IT environment currently utilizes both Linux and Windows operating systems. Consequently, both *ext* and *NTFS* file systems are in use. The webservers and some of the application servers employ *ext*, while the rest of the application servers, the database servers and the end-users' PCs are configured to use *NTFS*. Network-attached storage (NAS) configured with RAID 5 is also used for fault-tolerant document storage. Although the IT team is conversant with *file systems*, the concepts of *cluster*, *distributed file system* and *NoSQL* are new to the group. Nevertheless, after a discussion with the trained IT team members, the entire group is able to understand these concepts and technologies.

ETI's current IT landscape comprises entirely of relational databases that employ the ACID database design principle. The IT team has no understanding of the BASE principle and is having trouble comprehending the CAP theorem. Some of the team members are unsure about the need and importance of these concepts with regards to Big Data dataset storage. Seeing this, the IT-trained employees try to ease their fellow team members' confusion by explaining that these concepts are only applicable to the storage of enormous amounts of data in a distributed fashion on a cluster. Clusters have become the obvious choice for storing very large volume of data due to their ability to support linear scalability by scaling out.

Since clusters are comprised of nodes connected via a network, communication failures that create silos or partitions of a cluster are inevitable. To address the partition issue, the BASE principle and CAP theorem are introduced. They further explain that any database following the BASE principle becomes more responsive to its clients, albeit the data being read may be inconsistent when compared to a database that follows the ACID principle. Having understood the BASE principle, the IT team more easily comprehends why a database implemented in a cluster has to choose between consistency and availability.

Although none of the existing relational databases use sharding, almost all relational databases are replicated for disaster recovery and operational reporting. To better understand the concepts of sharding and replication, the IT team goes through an exercise of how these concepts can be applied to the *insurance quote* data as a large number of quotes are created and accessed quickly. For sharding, the team believes that using the *type* (the insurance sector—*heath, building, marine* and *aviation*) of the insurance quote as sharding criteria will create a balanced set of data across multiple nodes, for queries are mostly executed within the same insurance sector, and inter-sector queries are rare. With regards to replication, the team is in favor of choosing a NoSQL database that implements the *peer-to-peer* replication strategy. The reason behind their decision is that the insurance quotes are created and retrieved quite frequently but seldom updated. Hence the chances of getting an inconsistent record are low. Considering this, the team favors read/write performance over consistency by choosing *peer-to-peer* replication.

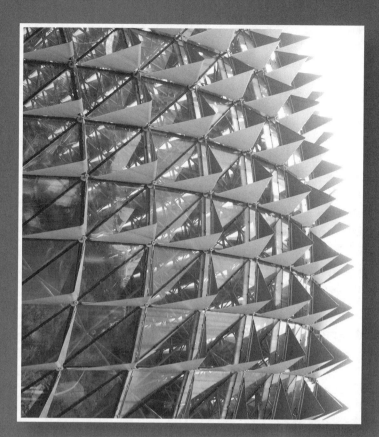

Chapter 6

Big Data Processing Concepts

The need to process large volumes of data is not new. When considering the relationship between a data warehouse and its associated data marts, it becomes clear that partitioning a large dataset into a smaller one can speed up processing. Big Data datasets stored on distributed file systems or within a distributed database are already partitioned into smaller datasets. The key to understanding Big Data processing is the realization that unlike the centralized processing, which occurs within a traditional relational database, Big Data is often processed in parallel in a distributed fashion at the location in which it is stored.

Of course, not all Big Data is batch-processed. Some data possesses the velocity characteristic and arrives in a time-ordered stream. Big Data analytics has answers for this type of processing as well. By leveraging in-memory storage architectures, sense-making can occur to deliver situational awareness. An important principle that constrains streaming Big Data processing is called the Speed, Consistency, and Volume (SCV) principle. It is detailed within this chapter as well.

To further the discussion of Big Data processing, each of the following concepts will be examined in turn:

- parallel data processing
- distributed data processing
- Hadoop
- processing workloads
- cluster

Parallel Data Processing

Parallel data processing involves the simultaneous execution of multiple sub-tasks that collectively comprise a larger task. The goal is to reduce the execution time by dividing a single larger task into multiple smaller tasks that run concurrently.

Although parallel data processing can be achieved through multiple networked machines, it is more typically achieved within the confines of a single machine with multiple processors or cores, as shown in Figure 6.1.

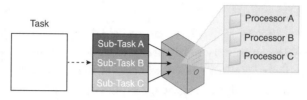

Figure 6.1

A task can be divided into three sub-tasks that are executed in parallel on three different processors within the same machine.

Distributed Data Processing

Distributed data processing is closely related to parallel data processing in that the same principle of "divide-and-conquer" is applied. However, distributed data processing is always achieved through physically separate machines that are networked together as a cluster. In Figure 6.2, a task is divided into three sub-tasks that are then executed on three different machines sharing one physical switch.

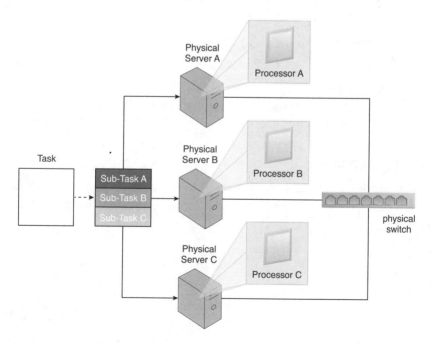

Figure 6.2

An example of distributed data processing.

Hadoop

Hadoop is an open-source framework for large-scale data storage and data processing that is compatible with commodity hardware. The Hadoop framework has established itself as a de facto industry platform for contemporary Big Data solutions. It can be used as an ETL engine or as an analytics engine for processing large amounts of structured, semi-structured and unstructured data. From an analysis perspective, Hadoop implements the MapReduce processing framework. Figure 6.3 illustrates some of Hadoop's features.

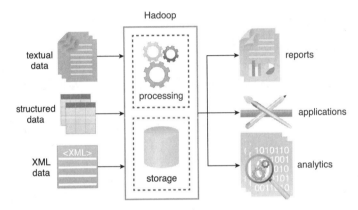

Figure 6.3
Hadoop is a versatile framework that provides both processing and storage capabilities.

Processing Workloads

A processing workload in Big Data is defined as the amount and nature of data that is processed within a certain amount of time. Workloads are usually divided into two types:

- batch
- transactional

Batch

Batch processing, also known as offline processing, involves processing data in batches and usually imposes delays, which in turn results in high-latency responses. Batch workloads typically involve large quantities of data with sequential read/writes and comprise of groups of read or write queries.

Queries can be complex and involve multiple joins. OLAP systems commonly process workloads in batches. Strategic BI and analytics are batch-oriented as they are highly read-intensive tasks involving large volumes of data. As shown in Figure 6.4, a batch workload comprises grouped read/writes that have a large data footprint and may contain complex joins and provide high-latency responses.

Figure 6.4

A batch workload can include grouped read/writes to INSERT, SELECT, UPDATE and DELETE.

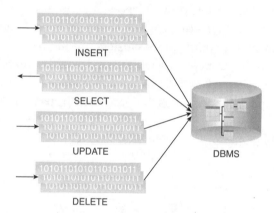

Transactional

Transactional processing is also known as online processing. Transactional workload processing follows an approach whereby data is processed interactively without delay, resulting in low-latency responses. Transaction workloads involve small amounts of data with random reads and writes.

OLTP and operational systems, which are generally write-intensive, fall within this category. Although these workloads contain a mix of read/write queries, they are generally more write-intensive than read-intensive.

Transactional workloads comprise random reads/writes that involve fewer joins than business intelligence and reporting workloads. Given their online nature and operational significance to the enterprise, they require low-latency responses with a smaller data footprint, as shown in Figure 6.5.

Figure 6.5

Transactional workloads
have few joins and lower
latency responses than
batch workloads.

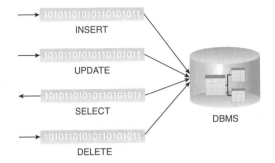

Cluster

In the same manner that clusters provide necessary support to create horizontally scalable storage solutions, clusters also provides the mechanism to enable distributed data processing with linear scalability. Since clusters are highly scalable, they provide an ideal environment for Big Data processing as large datasets can be divided into smaller datasets and then processed in parallel in a distributed manner. When leveraging a cluster, Big Data datasets can either be processed in batch mode or realtime mode (Figure 6.6). Ideally, a cluster will be comprised of low-cost commodity nodes that collectively provide increased processing capacity.

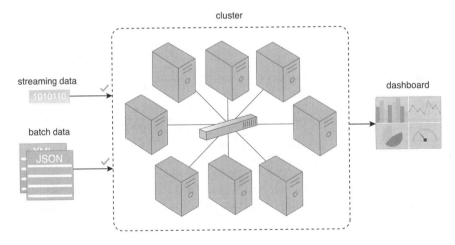

Figure 6.6

A cluster can be utilized to support batch processing of bulk data and realtime processing of streaming data.

An additional benefit of clusters is that they provide inherent redundancy and fault tolerance, as they consist of physically separate nodes. Redundancy and fault tolerance allow resilient processing and analysis to occur if a network or node failure occurs. Due to fluctuations in the processing demands placed upon a Big Data environment, leveraging cloud-host infrastructure services, or ready-made analytical environments as the backbone of a cluster, is sensible due to their elasticity and pay-for-use model of utility-based computing.

Processing in Batch Mode

In batch mode, data is processed offline in batches and the response time could vary from minutes to hours. As well, data must be persisted to the disk before it can be processed. Batch mode generally involves processing a range of large datasets, either on their own or joined together, essentially addressing the volume and variety characteristics of Big Data datasets.

The majority of Big Data processing occurs in batch mode. It is relatively simple, easy to set up and low in cost compared to realtime mode. Strategic BI, predictive and prescriptive analytics and ETL operations are commonly batch-oriented.

Batch Processing with MapReduce

MapReduce is a widely used implementation of a batch processing framework. It is highly scalable and reliable and is based on the principle of divide-and-conquer, which provides built-in fault tolerance and redundancy. It divides a big problem into a collection of smaller problems that can each be solved quickly. MapReduce has roots in both distributed and parallel computing. MapReduce is a batch-oriented processing engine (Figure 6.7) used to process large datasets using parallel processing deployed over clusters of commodity hardware.

Figure 6.7
The symbol used to represent a processing engine.

MapReduce does not require that the input data conform to any particular data model. Therefore, it can be used to process schema-less datasets. A dataset is broken down into multiple smaller parts, and operations are performed on each part independently and in parallel. The results from all operations are then summarized to arrive at the answer. Because of the coordination overhead involved in managing a job, the MapReduce processing engine generally only supports batch workloads as this work is not expected to have low latency. MapReduce is based on Google's research paper on the subject, published in early 2000.

The MapReduce processing engine works differently compared to the traditional data processing paradigm. Traditionally, data processing requires moving data from the storage node to the processing node that runs the data processing algorithm. This approach works fine for smaller datasets; however, with large datasets, moving data can incur more overhead than the actual processing of the data.

With MapReduce, the data processing algorithm is instead moved to the nodes that store the data. The data processing algorithm executes in parallel on these nodes, thereby eliminating the need to move the data first. This not only saves network bandwidth but it also results in a large reduction in processing time for large datasets, since processing smaller chunks of data in parallel is much faster.

Map and Reduce Tasks

A single processing run of the MapReduce processing engine is known as a MapReduce job. Each MapReduce job is composed of a map task and a reduce task and each task consists of multiple stages. Figure 6.8 shows the map and reduce task, along with their individual stages.

Map tasks

- map
- combine (optional)
- partition

Reduce tasks

- shuffle and sort
- reduce

Figure 6.8

An illustration of a MapReduce job with the map stage highlighted.

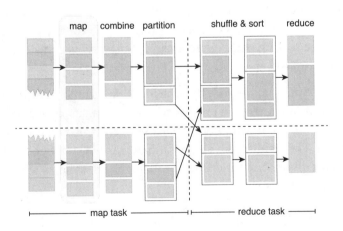

Map

The first stage of MapReduce is known as map, during which the dataset file is divided into multiple smaller splits. Each split is parsed into its constituent records as a key-value pair. The key is usually the ordinal position of the record, and the value is the actual record.

The parsed key-value pairs for each split are then sent to a map function or mapper, with one mapper function per split. The map function executes user-defined logic. Each split generally contains multiple key-value pairs, and the mapper is run once for each key-value pair in the split.

The mapper processes each key-value pair as per the user-defined logic and further generates a key-value pair as its output. The output key can either be the same as the input key or a substring value from the input value, or another serializable user-defined object. Similarly, the output value can either be the same as the input value or a substring value from the input value, or another serializable user-defined object.

When all records of the split have been processed, the output is a list of key-value pairs where multiple key-value pairs can exist for the same key. It should be noted that for an input key-value pair, a mapper may not produce any output key-value pair (filtering) or can generate multiple key-value pairs (demultiplexing.) The map stage can be summarized by the equation shown in Figure 6.9.

Figure 6.9

A summary of the map stage.

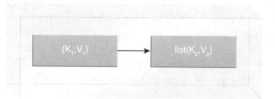

Combine

Generally, the output of the map function is handled directly by the reduce function. However, map tasks and reduce tasks are mostly run over different nodes. This requires moving data between mappers and reducers. This data movement can consume a lot of valuable bandwidth and directly contributes to processing latency.

With larger datasets, the time taken to move the data between map and reduce stages can exceed the actual processing undertaken by the map and reduce tasks. For this reason, the MapReduce engine provides an optional combine function (combiner) that summarizes a mapper's output before it gets processed by the reducer. Figure 6.10 illustrates the consolidation of the output from the map stage by the combine stage.

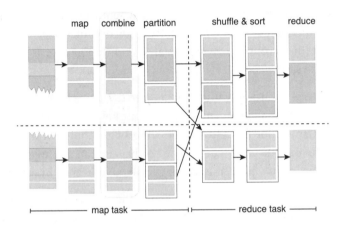

Figure 6.10

The combine stage groups the output from the map stage.

A combiner is essentially a reducer function that locally groups a mapper's output on the same node as the mapper. A reducer function can be used as a combiner function, or a custom user-defined function can be used.

The MapReduce engine combines all values for a given key from the mapper output, creating multiple key-value pairs as input to the combiner where the key is not repeated and the value exists as a list of all corresponding values for that key. The combiner stage is only an optimization stage, and may therefore not even be called by the MapReduce engine.

For example, a combiner function will work for finding the largest or the smallest number, but will not work for finding the average of all numbers since it only works with a subset of the data. The combine stage can be summarized by the equation shown in Figure 6.11.

Figure 6.11

A summary of the combine stage.

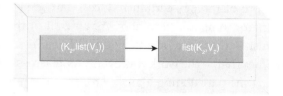

Partition

During the partition stage, if more than one reducer is involved, a partitioner divides the output from the mapper or combiner (if specified and called by the MapReduce engine) into partitions between reducer instances. The number of partitions will equal the number of reducers. Figure 6.12 shows the partition stage assigning the outputs from the combine stage to specific reducers.

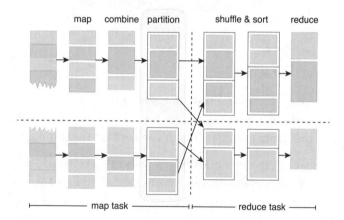

Figure 6.12

The partition stage assigns output from the map task to reducers.

Although each partition contains multiple key-value pairs, all records for a particular key are assigned to the same partition. The MapReduce engine guarantees a random and fair distribution between reducers while making sure that all of the same keys across multiple mappers end up with the same reducer instance.

Depending on the nature of the job, certain reducers can sometimes receive a large number of key-value pairs compared to others. As a result of this uneven workload, some reducers will finish earlier than others. Overall, this is less efficient and leads to longer job execution times than if the work was evenly split across reducers. This can be rectified by customizing the partitioning logic in order to guarantee a fair distribution of key-value pairs.

The partition function is the last stage of the map task. It returns the index of the reducer to which a particular partition should be sent. The partition stage can be summarized by the equation in Figure 6.13.

Figure 6.13

A summary of the partition stage.

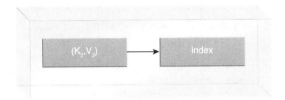

Shuffle and Sort

During the first stage of the reduce task, output from all partitioners is copied across the network to the nodes running the reduce task. This is known as shuffling. The list based key-value output from each partitioner can contain the same key multiple times.

Next, the MapReduce engine automatically groups and sorts the key-value pairs according to the keys so that the output contains a sorted list of all input keys and their values with the same keys appearing together. The way in which keys are grouped and sorted can be customized.

This merge creates a single key-value pair per group, where key is the group key and the value is the list of all group values. This stage can be summarized by the equation in Figure 6.14.

Figure 6.15 depicts a hypothetical MapReduce job that is executing the shuffle and sort stage of the reduce task.

Figure 6.14

A summary of the shuffle and sort stage.

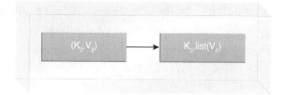

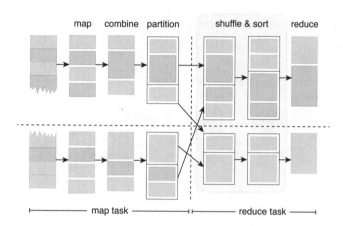

Figure 6.15

During the shuffle and sort stage, data is copied across the network to the reducer nodes and sorted by key.

Reduce

Reduce is the final stage of the reduce task. Depending on the user-defined logic specified in the reduce function (reducer), the reducer will either further summarize its input or will emit the output without making any changes. In either case, for each key-value pair that a reducer receives, the list of values stored in the value part of the pair is processed and another key-value pair is written out.

The output key can either be the same as the input key or a substring value from the input value, or another serializable user-defined object. The output value can either be the same as the input value or a substring value from the input value, or another serializable user-defined object.

Note that just like the mapper, for the input key-value pair, a reducer may not produce any output key-value pair (filtering) or can generate multiple key-value pairs (demultiplexing). The output of the reducer, that is the key-value pairs, is then written out as a separate file—one file per reducer. This is depicted in Figure 6.16, which highlights the reduce stage of the reduce task. To view the full output from the MapReduce job, all the file parts must be combined.

The number of reducers can be customized. It is also possible to have a MapReduce job without a reducer, for example when performing filtering.

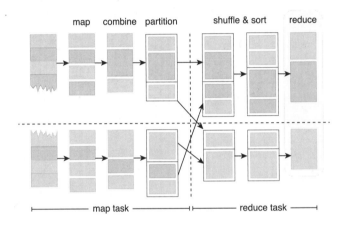

Figure 6.16
The reduce stage is the last stage of the reduce task.

Note that the output signature (key-value types) of the map function should match that of the input signature (key-value types) of the reduce/combine function. The reduce stage can be summarized by the equation in Figure 6.17.

Figure 6.17
A summary of the
reduce stage.

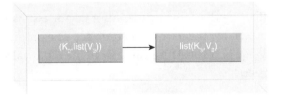

A Simple MapReduce Example

The following steps are shown in Figure 6.18:

1. The input (sales.txt) is divided into two splits.

2. Two map tasks running on two different nodes, Node A and Node B, extract product and quantity from the respective split's records in parallel. The output from each map function is a key-value pair where product is the key while quantity is the value.

3. The combiner then performs local summation of product quantities.

4. As there is only one reduce task, no partitioning is performed.

5. The output from the two map tasks is then copied to a third node, Node C, that runs the shuffle stage as part of the reduce task.

6. The sort stage then groups all quantities of the same product together as a list.

7. Like the combiner, the reduce function then sums up the quantities of each unique product in order to create the output.

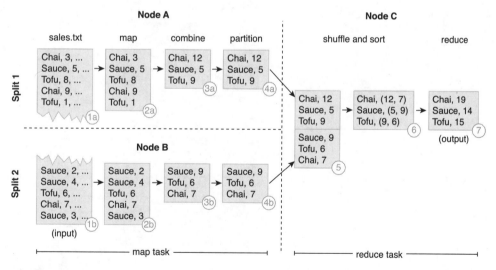

Figure 6.18

An example of MapReduce in action.

Understanding MapReduce Algorithms

Unlike traditional programming models, MapReduce follows a distinct programming model. In order to understand how algorithms can be designed or adapted to this programming model, its design principle first needs to be explored.

As described earlier, MapReduce works on the principle of divide-and-conquer. However, it is important to understand the semantics of this principle in the context of MapReduce. The divide-and-conquer principle is generally achieved using one of the following approaches:

- *Task Parallelism* – Task parallelism refers to the parallelization of data processing by dividing a task into sub-tasks and running each sub-task on a separate processor, generally on a separate node in a cluster (Figure 6.19). Each sub-task generally executes a different algorithm, with its own copy of the same data or different data as its input, in parallel. Generally, the output from multiple sub-tasks is joined together to obtain the final set of results.

Figure 6.19

A task is split into two sub-tasks, Sub-task A and Sub-task B, which are then run on two different nodes on the same dataset.

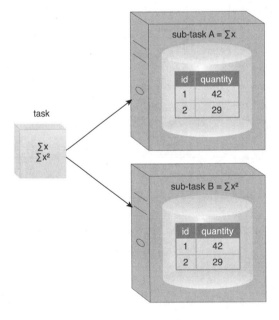

- *Data Parallelism* – Data parallelism refers to the parallelization of data processing by dividing a dataset into multiple datasets and processing each sub-dataset in parallel (Figure 6.20). The sub-datasets are spread across multiple nodes and are all processed using the same algorithm. Generally, the output from each processed sub-dataset is joined together to obtain the final set of results.

Figure 6.20

A dataset is divided into two sub-datasets, Sub-dataset A and Sub-dataset B, which are then processed on two different nodes using the same function.

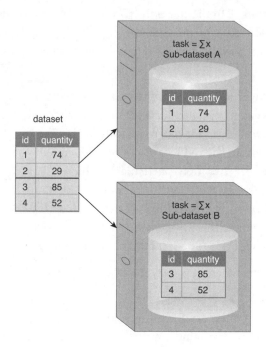

Within Big Data environments, the same task generally needs to be performed repeatedly on a data unit, such as a record, where the complete dataset is distributed across multiple locations due to its large size. MapReduce addresses this requirement by employing the data parallelism approach, where the data is divided into splits. Each split is then processed by its own instance of the map function, which contains the same processing logic as the other map functions.

The majority of traditional algorithmic development follows a sequential approach where operations on data are performed one after the other in such a way that subsequent operation is dependent on its preceding operation.

In MapReduce, operations are divided among the map and reduce functions. Map and reduce tasks are independent and in turn run isolated from one another. Furthermore, each instance of a map or reduce function runs independently of other instances.

Function signatures in traditional algorithmic development are generally not constrained. In MapReduce, the map and reduce function signatures are constrained to a set of key-value pairs. This is the only way that a map function can communicate with a reduce function. Apart from this, the logic in the map function is dependent on how records are parsed, which further depends on what constitutes a logical data unit within the dataset.

For example, each line in a text file generally represents a single record. However, it may be that a set of two or more lines actually constitute a single record (Figure 6.21). Furthermore, the logic within the reduce function is dependent on the output of the map function, particularly which keys were emitted from the map function as the reduce function receives a unique key with a consolidated list of all of its values. It should be noted that in some scenarios, such as with text extraction, a reduce function may not be required.

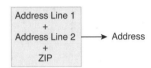

Figure 6.21

An instance where three lines constitute a single record.

The key considerations when developing a MapReduce algorithm can be summarized as follows:

- Use of relatively simplistic algorithmic logic, such that the required result can be obtained by applying the same logic to different portions of a dataset in parallel and then aggregating the results in some manner.

- Availability of the dataset in a distributed manner partitioned across a cluster so that multiple map functions can process different subsets of a dataset in parallel.

- Understanding of the data structure within the dataset so that a meaningful data unit (a single record) can be chosen.

- Dividing algorithmic logic into map and reduce functions so that the logic in the map function is not dependent on the complete dataset, since only data within a single split is available.

- Emitting the correct key from the map function along with all the required data as value because the reduce function's logic can only process those values that were emitted as part of the key-value pairs from the map function.

- Emitting the correct key from the reduce function along with the required data as value because the output from each reduce function becomes the final output of the MapReduce algorithm.

Processing in Realtime Mode

In realtime mode, data is processed in-memory as it is captured before being persisted to the disk. Response time generally ranges from a sub-second to under a minute. Realtime mode addresses the velocity characteristic of Big Data datasets.

Within Big Data processing, realtime processing is also called event or stream processing as the data either arrives continuously (stream) or at intervals (event). The individual event/stream datum is generally small in size, but its continuous nature results in very large datasets.

Another related term, interactive mode, falls within the category of realtime. Interactive mode generally refers to query processing in realtime. Operational BI/analytics are generally conducted in realtime mode.

A fundamental principle related to Big Data processing is called the Speed, Consistency and Volume (SCV) principle. It is covered first as it establishes some basic constraints on processing that mainly impact realtime processing mode.

Speed Consistency Volume (SCV)

Whereas the CAP theorem is primarily related to distributed data storage, the SCV (Figure 6.22) principle is related to distributed data processing. It states that a distributed data processing system can be designed to support only two of the following three requirements:

- *Speed* – Speed refers to how quickly the data can be processed once it is generated. In the case of realtime analytics, data is processed comparatively faster than batch analytics. This generally excludes the time taken to capture data and focuses only on the actual data processing, such as generating statistics or executing an algorithm.

- *Consistency* – Consistency refers to the accuracy and the precision of the results. Results are deemed accurate if they are close to the correct value and precise if close to each other. A more consistent system will make use of all available data, resulting in high accuracy and precision as compared to a less consistent system that makes use of sampling techniques, which can result in lower accuracy with an acceptable level of precision.

- *Volume* – Volume refers to the amount of data that can be processed. Big Data's velocity characteristic results in fast growing datasets leading to huge volumes of data that need to be processed in a distributed manner. Processing such voluminous data in its entirety while ensuring speed and consistency is not possible.

If speed (S) and consistency (C) are required, it is not possible to process high volumes of data (V) because large amounts of data slow down data processing.

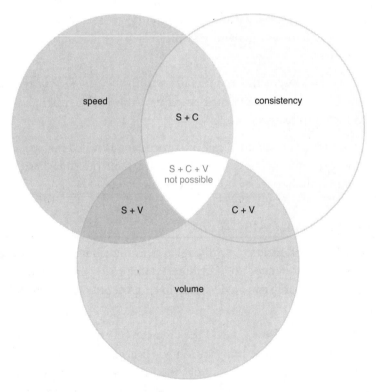

Figure 6.22
This Venn diagram summarizes the SCV principle.

If consistency (C) and processing of high volumes of data (V) are required, it is not possible to process the data at high speed (S) as achieving high speed data processing requires smaller data volumes.

If high volume (V) data processing coupled with high speed (S) data processing is required, the processed results will not be consistent (C) since high-speed processing of large amounts of data involves sampling the data, which may reduce consistency.

It should be noted that the choice of which two of the three dimensions to support is fully dependent upon the system requirements of the analysis environment.

In Big Data environments, making the maximum amount of data available is mandatory for performing in-depth analysis, such as pattern identification. Hence, forgoing volume (V) over speed (S) and consistency (C) needs to be considered carefully as data may still be required for batch processing in order to glean further insights.

In the case of Big Data processing, assuming that data (V) loss is unacceptable, generally a realtime data analysis system will either be S+V or C+V, depending upon whether speed (S) or consistent results (C) is favored.

Processing Big Data in realtime generally refers to realtime or near-realtime analytics. Data is processed as it arrives at the enterprise boundary without an unreasonable delay. Instead of initially persisting the data to the disk, for example to a database, the data is first processed in memory and then persisted to the disk for future use or archival purposes. This is opposite of batch processing mode, where data is persisted to the disk first and then subsequently processed, which can create significant delays.

Analyzing Big Data in realtime requires the use of in-memory storage devices (IMDGs or IMDBs). Once in memory, the data can then be processed in realtime without incurring any hard-disk I/O latency. The realtime processing may involve calculating simple statistics, executing complex algorithms or updating the state of the in-memory data as a result of a change detected in some metric.

For enhanced data analysis, in-memory data can be combined with previously batch-processed data or denormalized data loaded from on-disk storage devices. This helps to achieve realtime data processing as datasets can be joined in memory.

Although realtime Big Data processing generally refers to incoming new data, it can also include performing queries on previously persisted data that requires interactive response. Once the data has been processed, the processing results can then be published for interested consumers. This may occur via a realtime dashboard application or a Web application that delivers realtime updates to the user.

Depending on system requirements, the processed data along with the raw input data can be offloaded to on-disk storage for subsequent complex, batch data analyses.

The following steps are shown in Figure 6.23:

1. Streaming data is captured via a data transfer engine.

2. It is then simultaneously saved to an in-memory storage device (a) and an on-disk storage device (b).

3. A processing engine is then used to process data in realtime.

4. Finally, the results are fed to a dashboard for operational analysis.

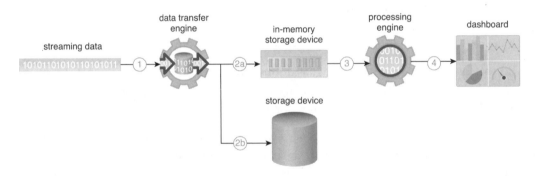

Figure 6.23
An example of realtime data processing in a Big Data environment.

Two important concepts related to realtime Big Data processing are:

• Event Stream Processing (ESP)

• Complex Event Processing (CEP)

Event Stream Processing

During ESP, an incoming stream of events, generally from a single source and ordered by time, is continuously analyzed. The analysis can occur via simple queries or the application of algorithms that are mostly formula-based. The analysis takes place in-memory before storing the events to an on-disk storage device.

Other (memory resident) data sources can also be incorporated into the analysis for performing richer analytics. The processing results can be fed to a dashboard or can act as a trigger for another application to perform a preconfigured action or further analysis. ESP focuses more on speed than complexity; the operation to be executed is comparatively simple to aid faster execution.

Complex Event Processing

During CEP, a number of realtime events often coming from disparate sources and arriving at different time intervals are analyzed simultaneously for the detection of patterns and initiation of action. Rule-based algorithms and statistical techniques are applied, taking into account business logic and process context to discover cross-cutting complex event patterns.

CEP focuses more on complexity, providing rich analytics. However, as a result, speed of execution may be adversely affected. In general, CEP is considered to be a superset of ESP and often the output of ESP results in the generation of synthetic events that can be fed into CEP.

Realtime Big Data Processing and SCV

While designing a realtime Big Data processing system, the SCV principle needs to be kept in mind. In light of this principle, consider a hard-realtime and a near-realtime Big Data processing system. For both hard-realtime and near-realtime scenarios, we assume that data loss is unacceptable; in other words, high data volume (V) processing is required for both the systems.

Note that the requirement that the data loss should not occur does not mean that all data will actually be processed in realtime. Rather, it means that the system captures all input data and that the data is always persisted to disk either directly by writing it to on-disk storage or indirectly to a disk serving as a persistence layer for in-memory storage.

In the case of a hard-realtime system, a fast response (S) is required, hence consistency (C) will be compromised if high volume data (V) needs to be processed in memory. This scenario will require the use of sampling or approximation techniques, which will in turn generate less accurate results but with tolerable precision in a timely manner.

In the case of a near-realtime system, a reasonably fast response (S) is required, hence consistency (C) can be guaranteed if high volume data (V) needs to be processed in memory. Results will be more accurate when compared to a hard-realtime system since the complete dataset can be used instead of taking samples or employing approximation techniques.

Thus, in the context of Big Data processing, a hard-realtime system requires a compromise on consistency (C) to guarantee a fast response (S) while a near-realtime system can compromise speed (S) to guarantee consistent results (C).

Realtime Big Data Processing and MapReduce

MapReduce is generally unsuitable for realtime Big Data processing. There are several reasons for this, not the least of which is the amount of overhead associated with MapReduce job creation and coordination. MapReduce is intended for the batch-oriented processing of large amounts of data that has been stored to disk. MapReduce cannot process data incrementally and can only process complete datasets. It therefore requires all input data to be available in its entirety before the execution of the data processing job. This is at odds with the requirements for realtime data processing as realtime processing involves data that is often incomplete and continuously arriving via a stream.

Additionally, with MapReduce a reduce task cannot generally start before the completion of all map tasks. First, the map output is persisted locally on each node that runs the map function. Next, the map output is copied over the network to the nodes that run the reduce function, introducing processing latency. Similarly, the results of one reducer cannot be directly fed into another reducer, rather the results would have to be passed to a mapper first in a subsequent MapReduce job.

As demonstrated, MapReduce is generally not useful for realtime processing, especially when hard-realtime constraints are present. There are however some strategies that can enable the use of MapReduce in near-realtime Big Data processing scenarios.

One strategy is to use in-memory storage to store data that serves as input to interactive queries that consist of MapReduce jobs. Alternatively, micro-batch MapReduce jobs can be deployed that are configured to run on comparatively smaller datasets at frequent intervals, such as every fifteen minutes. Another approach is to continuously run MapReduce jobs against on-disk datasets to create materialized views that can then be combined with small volume analysis results, obtained from newly arriving in-memory streaming data, for interactive query processing.

Given the predominance of smart devices and corporate desires to engage customers more proactively, advancements in realtime Big Data processing capabilities are occurring very quickly. Several open source Apache projects, specifically Spark, Storm and Tez, provide true realtime Big Data processing capabilities and are the foundation of a new generation of realtime processing solutions.

CASE STUDY EXAMPLE

Most of ETI's operational information systems utilize client-server and n-tier architectures. After surveying its inventory of IT systems, the company determines that none of the systems employ distributed data processing. Instead, data that needs to be processed is either received from a client or retrieved from the database and then processed by a single machine. Although the current data processing model does not employ distributed data processing, some of the software engineers agree that the parallel data processing model on a machine-level is used to some degree. Their understanding is based on the fact that some of their high-performance custom applications make use of multi-threading to enable a data processing job to be split for execution on the multiple cores present in rack-based servers.

Processing Workloads

The IT team understands *transactional* and *batch* workloads because both workloads are currently manifested in data processing in ETI's IT environment. Operational systems, such as claims management and billing, exhibit *transactional workload* comprising of ACID-compliant database transactions. On the other hand, the population of the EDW via ETL and BI activities represents *batch workload*.

Processing in Batch Mode

Being new to Big Data technologies, the IT team opts for an incremental approach by first implementing batch processing of data. Once the team has gained enough experience, it can move toward implementing realtime processing of data.

To get an understanding of the MapReduce framework, the IT team picks up a scenario where MapReduce can be applied, and performs a mental exercise. The members observe that one task that needs to be performed on a regular basis and takes a long time to complete is the locating of the most popular insurance products. The popularity of an insurance product is determined by finding out how many times the corresponding page of that product was viewed. The webserver creates an entry (a line of text with a comma-delimited set of fields) in a log file whenever a webpage is requested. Among other fields, the webserver log contains the *IP address* of the website visitor that requested the webpage, the *time* when the webpage was requested and the *page name*. The *page name* corresponds to the name of the insurance product that the website visitor is interested in. Currently, the webserver logs are imported from all webservers into a relational database. Next an SQL query is executed to get a list of page names along with a count of page views. The import of the log files and the execution of the SQL query take a long time to complete.

To obtain the page view count using MapReduce, the IT team takes the following approach. In the *map* stage, for each input line of text, the *page name* is extracted and set as the output key while a numeric value of *1* is set as the value. In the *reduce* stage, all of the input values (a list of *1s*) for a single input key (the *page name*) are simply summed up using a loop to get the *total* page view count. The output from the *reduce* stage consists of the *page name* as the key and the *total* page view count as the value. To make the processing more efficient, the trained IT team members remind the rest of the group that a *combiner* can be used to execute exactly the same logic as the *reducer*. However, the output from the combiner will consist of the subtotal of the page views count. Therefore, in the reducer, although the logic for getting the total number of page views remains the same, instead of getting a list of *1s* (the value) against each *page name* (the key), the list of input values will consist of the subtotal from each *mapper*.

Processing in Realtime

The IT team believes that the *event stream processing* model can be used to perform sentiment analysis on Twitter data in realtime to find the reasons behind any customer dissatisfaction.

Chapter 7

Big Data Storage Technology

On-Disk Storage Devices

In-Memory Storage Devices

Storage technology has continued to evolve over time, moving from inside the server to out on the network. Today's push to converged architecture puts compute, storage, memory and network back into the box, where the architecture can be uniformly administered. Amidst these changes, the need to store Big Data has radically altered the relational, database-centric view that has been embraced by Enterprise ICT since the late 1980s. The bottom line is that relational technology is simply not scalable in a manner to support Big Data volumes. Not to mention, businesses can find genuine value in processing semi-structured and unstructured data, which are generally incompatible with relational approaches.

Big Data has pushed the storage boundary to unified views of the available memory and disk storage of a cluster. If more storage is needed, horizontal scalability allows the expansion of the cluster through the addition of more nodes. The fact that this is equally true for both memory and disk devices is important as innovative approaches deliver realtime analytics via in-memory storage. Even batch-based processing has accelerated by the performance of Solid State Drives (SSDs), which have become less expensive.

This chapter delves deeper into the use of on-disk and in-memory storage devices for Big Data. Topics ranging from simple notions of distributed files systems for flat file storage to NoSQL devices for unstructured and semi-structured data are covered. Specifically, the different varieties of NoSQL database technologies and their appropriate uses are explained. The last major topic of the chapter is in-memory storage, which facilitates the processing of streaming data and can hold entire databases. These technologies enable a shift from traditional on-disk, batch-oriented processing to in-memory realtime processing.

On-Disk Storage Devices

On-disk storage generally utilizes low cost hard-disk drives for long-term storage. On-disk storage can be implemented via a distributed file system or a database as shown in Figure 7.1.

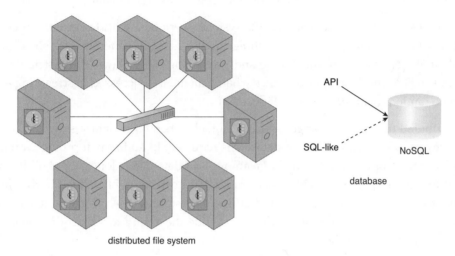

distributed file system

Figure 7.1
On-disk storage can be implemented with a distributed file system or a database.

Distributed File Systems

Distributed file systems, like any file system, are agnostic to the data being stored and therefore support schema-less data storage. In general, a distributed file system storage device provides out of box redundancy and high availability by copying data to multiple locations via replication.

A storage device that is implemented with a distributed file system provides simple, fast access data storage that is capable of storing large datasets that are non-relational in nature, such as semi-structured and unstructured data. Although based on straightforward file locking mechanisms for concurrency control, it provides fast read/write capability, which addresses the velocity characteristic of Big Data.

A distributed file system is not ideal for datasets comprising a large number of small files as this creates excessive disk-seek activity, slowing down the overall data access. There is also more overhead involved in processing multiple smaller files, as dedicated processes are generally spawned by the processing engine at runtime for processing each file before the results are synchronized from across the cluster.

Due to these limitations, distributed file systems work best with fewer but larger files accessed in a sequential manner. Multiple smaller files are generally combined into a single file to enable optimum storage and processing. This allows the distributed file systems to have increased performance when data must be accessed in streaming mode with no random reads and writes (Figure 7.2).

A distributed file system storage device is suitable when large datasets of raw data are to be stored or when archiving of datasets is required. In addition, it provides an inexpensive storage option for storing large amounts of data over a long period of time that needs to remain online. This is because more disks can simply be added to the cluster without needing to offload the data to offline data storage, such as tapes. It should be noted that distributed file systems do not provide the ability to search the contents of files as standard out-of-the-box capability.

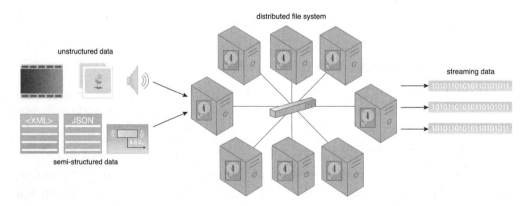

Figure 7.2
A distributed file system accessing data in streaming mode with no random reads and writes.

RDBMS Databases

Relational database management systems (RDBMSs) are good for handling transactional workloads involving small amounts of data with random read/write properties. RDBMSs are ACID-compliant, and, to honor this compliance, they are generally restricted to a single node. For this reason, RDBMSs do not provide out-of-the-box redundancy and fault tolerance.

To handle large volumes of data arriving at a fast pace, relational databases generally need to scale. RDBMSs employ vertical scaling, not horizontal scaling, which is a more costly and disruptive scaling strategy. This makes RDBMSs less than ideal for long-term storage of data that accumulates over time.

Note that some relational databases, for example IBM DB2 pureScale, Sybase ASE Cluster Edition, Oracle Real Application Clusters (RAC) and Microsoft Parallel Data Warehouse (PDW), are capable of being run on clusters (Figure 7.3). However, these database clusters still use shared storage that can act as a single point of failure.

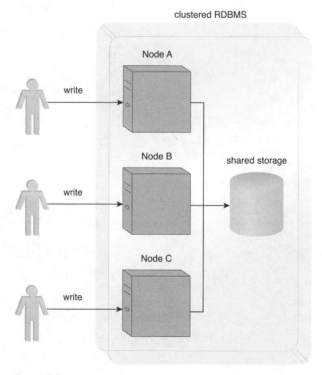

Figure 7.3
A clustered rational database uses a shared storage architecture, which is a potential single point of failure that affects the availability of the database.

Relational databases need to be manually sharded, mostly using application logic. This means that the application logic needs to know which shard to query in order to get the required data. This further complicates data processing when data from multiple shards is required.

The following steps are shown in Figure 7.4:

1. A user writes a record (id = 2).

2. The application logic determines which shard it should be written to.

3. It is sent to the shard determined by the application logic.

4. The user reads a record (id = 4), and the application logic determines which shard contains the data.

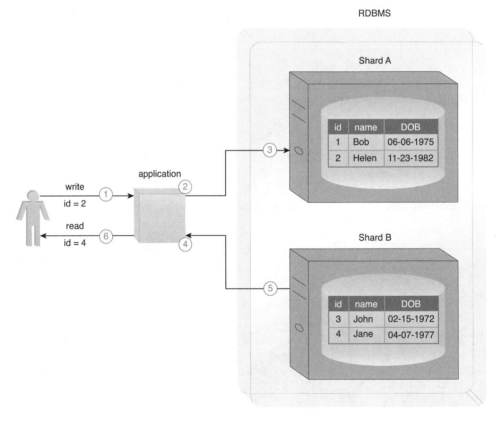

Figure 7.4
A relational database is manually sharded using application logic.

5. The data is read and returned to the application.

6. The application then returns the record to the user.

The following steps are shown in Figure 7.5:

1. A user requests multiple records (id = 1, 3) and the application logic is used to determine which shards need to be read.

2. It is determined by the application logic that both Shard A and Shard B need to be read.

3. The data is read and joined by the application.

4. Finally, the data is returned to the user.

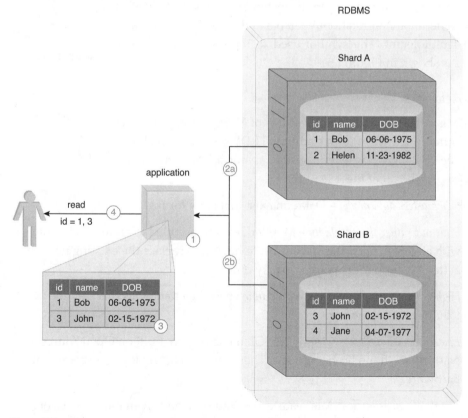

Figure 7.5

An example of the use of the application logic to join data retrieved from multiple shards.

Relational databases generally require data to adhere to a schema. As a result, storage of semi-structured and unstructured data whose schemas are non-relational is not directly supported. Furthermore, with a relational database schema conformance is validated at the time of data insert or update by checking the data against the constraints of the schema. This introduces overhead that creates latency.

This latency makes relational databases a less than ideal choice for storing high velocity data that needs a highly available database storage device with fast data write capability. As a result of its shortcomings, a traditional RDBMS is generally not useful as the primary storage device in a Big Data solution environment.

NoSQL Databases

Not-only SQL (NoSQL) refers to technologies used to develop next generation non-relational databases that are highly scalable and fault-tolerant. The symbol used to represent NoSQL databases is shown in Figure 7.6.

NoSQL Database

Characteristics

Below is a list of the principal features of NoSQL storage devices that differentiate them from traditional RDBMSs. This list should only be considered a general guide, as not all NoSQL storage devices exhibit all of these features.

Figure 7.6
The symbol used to represent a NoSQL database.

- *Schema-less data model* – Data can exist in its raw form.

- *Scale out rather than scale up* – More nodes can be added to obtain additional storage with a NoSQL database, in contrast to having to replace the existing node with a better, higher performance/capacity one.

- *Highly available* – This is built on cluster-based technologies that provide fault tolerance out of the box.

- *Lower operational costs* – Many NoSQL databases are built on Open Source platforms with no licensing costs. They can often be deployed on commodity hardware.

- *Eventual consistency* – Data reads across multiple nodes but may not be consistent immediately after a write. However, all nodes will eventually be in a consistent state.

- *BASE, not ACID* – BASE compliance requires a database to maintain high availability in the event of network/node failure, while not requiring the database to be in a consistent state whenever an update occurs. The database can be in a soft/inconsistent state until it eventually attains consistency. As a result, in consideration of the CAP theorem, NoSQL storage devices are generally AP or CP.

- *API driven data access* – Data access is generally supported via API based queries, including RESTful APIs, whereas some implementations may also provide SQL-like query capability.

- *Auto sharding and replication* – To support horizontal scaling and provide high availability, a NoSQL storage device automatically employs sharding and replication techniques where the dataset is partitioned horizontally and then copied to multiple nodes.

- *Integrated caching* – This removes the need for a third-party distributed caching layer, such as Memcached.

- *Distributed query support* – NoSQL storage devices maintain consistent query behavior across multiple shards.

- *Polyglot persistence* – The use of NoSQL storage does not mandate retiring traditional RDBMSs. In fact, both can be used at the same time, thereby supporting polyglot persistence, which is an approach of persisting data using different types of storage technologies within the same solution architecture. This is good for developing systems requiring structured as well as semi/unstructured data.

- *Aggregate-focused* – Unlike relational databases that are most effective with fully normalized data, NoSQL storage devices store de-normalized aggregated data (an entity containing merged, often nested, data for an object) thereby eliminating the need for joins and extensive mapping between application objects and the data stored in the database. One exception, however, is that graph database storage devices (introduced shortly) are not aggregate-focused.

Rationale

The emergence of NoSQL storage devices can primarily be attributed to the volume, velocity and variety characteristics of Big Data datasets.

Volume

The storage requirement of ever increasing data volumes commands the use of databases that are highly scalable while keeping costs down for the business to remain competitive. NoSQL storage devices fulfill this requirement by providing scale out capability while using inexpensive commodity servers.

Velocity

The fast influx of data requires databases with fast access data write capability. NoSQL storage devices enable fast writes by using schema-on-read rather than schema-on-write principle. Being highly available, NoSQL storage devices can ensure that write latency does not occur because of node or network failure.

Variety

A storage device needs to handle different data formats including documents, emails, images and videos and incomplete data. NoSQL storage devices can store these different forms of semi-structured and unstructured data formats. At the same time, NoSQL storage devices are able to store schema-less data and incomplete data with the added ability of making schema changes as the data model of the datasets evolve. In other words, NoSQL databases support *schema evolution*.

Types

NoSQL storage devices can mainly be divided into four types based on the way they store data, as shown in Figures 7.7–7.10:

- key-value
- document
- column-family
- graph

Figure 7.7

An example of key-value NoSQL storage.

key	value
631	John Smith, 10.0.30.25, Good customer service
365	100101011101101111011101010110101010011100011010
198	<CustomerId>32195</CustomerId><Total>43.25</Total>

Figure 7.8

An example of document NoSQL storage.

```
{
    invoiceId:37235,
    date:19600801,
    custId:29317,
    items:[
        {itemId:473,quantity:2},
        {itemId:971,quantity:5}
    ]
}
```

Figure 7.9

An example of column-family NoSQL storage.

studentId	personal details	address	modules history
821	FirstName: Cristie LastName: Augustin DoB: 03-15-1992 Gender: Female Ethnicity: French	Street: 123 New Ave City: Portland State: Oregon ZipCode: 12345 Country: USA	Taken: 5 Passed: 4 Failed: 1
742	FirstName: Carlos LastName: Rodriguez MiddleName: Jose Gender: Male	Street: 456 Old Ave City: Los Angeles Country: USA	Taken: 7 Passed: 5 Failed: 2

Figure 7.10

An example of graph NoSQL storage.

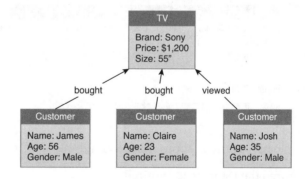

Key-Value

Key-value storage devices store data as key-value pairs and act like hash tables. The table is a list of values where each value is identified by a key. The value is opaque to the database and is typically stored as a BLOB. The value stored can be any aggregate, ranging from sensor data to videos.

Value look-up can only be performed via the keys as the database is oblivious to the details of the stored aggregate. Partial updates are not possible. An update is either a delete or an insert operation.

Key-value storage devices generally do not maintain any indexes, therefore writes are quite fast. Based on a simple storage model, key-value storage devices are highly scalable.

As keys are the only means of retrieving the data, the key is usually appended with the type of the value being saved for easy retrieval. An example of this is *123_sensor1*.

To provide some structure to the stored data, most key-value storage devices provide collections or buckets (like tables) into which key-value pairs can be organized. A single collection can hold multiple data formats, as shown in Figure 7.11. Some implementations support compressing values for reducing the storage footprint. However, this introduces latency at read time, as the data needs to be decompressed first before being returned.

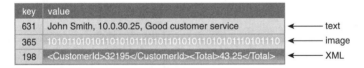

Figure 7.11
An example of data organized into key-value pairs.

A key-value storage device is appropriate when:

- unstructured data storage is required

- high performance read/writes are required

- the value is fully identifiable via the key alone

- value is a standalone entity that is not dependent on other values

- values have a comparatively simple structure or are binary

- query patterns are simple, involving insert, select and delete operations only

- stored values are manipulated at the application layer

A key-value storage device is inappropriate when:

- applications require searching or filtering data using attributes of the stored value

- relationships exist between different key-value entries

- a group of keys' values need to be updated in a single transaction

- multiple keys require manipulation in a single operation

- schema consistency across different values is required

- update to individual attributes of the value is required

Examples of key-value storage devices include Riak, Redis, and Amazon Dynamo DB.

Document

Document storage devices also store data as key-value pairs. However, unlike key-value storage devices, the stored value is a document that can be queried by the database. These documents can have a complex nested structure, such as an invoice, as shown in Figure 7.12. The documents can be encoded using either a text-based encoding scheme, such as XML or JSON, or using a binary encoding scheme, such as BSON (Binary JSON).

Like key-value storage devices, most document storage devices provide collections or buckets (like tables) into which key-value pairs can be organized. The main differences between document storage devices and key-value storage devices are as follows:

- document storage devices are value-aware

- the stored value is self-describing; the schema can be inferred from the structure of the value or a reference to the schema for the document is included in the value

- a select operation can reference a field inside the aggregate value

- a select operation can retrieve a part of the aggregate value

- partial updates are supported; therefore a subset of the aggregate can be updated

- indexes that speed up searches are generally supported

Each document can have a different schema; therefore, it is possible to store different types of documents in the same collection or bucket. Additional fields can be added to a document after the initial insert, thereby providing flexible schema support.

It should be noted that document storage devices are not limited to storing data that occurs in the form of actual documents, such as an XML file, but they can also be used to store any aggregate that consists of a collection of fields having a flat or a nested schema. See Figure 7.12, which shows JSON documents being stored in a document NoSQL database.

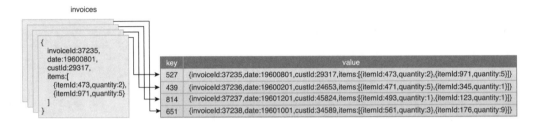

Figure 7.12
A depiction of JSON data stored in a document storage device.

A document storage device is appropriate when:

- storing semi-structured document-oriented data comprising flat or nested schema

- schema evolution is a requirement as the structure of the document is either unknown or is likely to change

- applications require a partial update of the aggregate stored as a document

- searches need to be performed on different fields of the documents

- storing domain objects, such as customers, in serialized object form

- query patterns involve insert, select, update and delete operations

A document storage device is inappropriate when:

- multiple documents need to be updated as part of a single transaction

- performing operations that need joins between multiple documents or storing data that is normalized

- schema enforcement for achieving consistent query design is required as the document structure may change between successive query runs, which will require restructuring the query

- the stored value is not self-describing and does not have a reference to a schema

- binary data needs to be stored

Examples of document storage devices include MongoDB, CouchDB, and Terrastore.

Column-Family

Column-family storage devices store data much like a traditional RDBMS but group related columns together in a row, resulting in column-families (Figure 7.13). Each column can be a collection of related columns itself, referred to as a super-column.

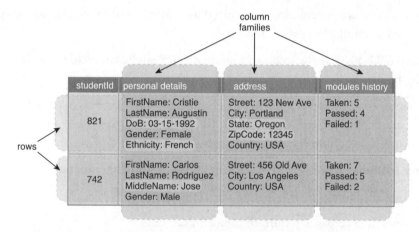

Figure 7.13

The highlighted columns depict the flexible schema feature supported by the column-family databases, where each row can have a different set of columns.

Each super-column can contain an arbitrary number of related columns that are generally retrieved or updated as a single unit. Each row consists of multiple column-families and can have a different set of columns, thereby manifesting flexible schema support. Each row is identified by a row key.

Column-family storage devices provide fast data access with random read/write capability. They store different column-families in separate physical files, which improves query responsiveness as only the required column-families are searched.

Some column-family storage devices provide support for selectively compressing column-families. Leaving searchable column-families uncompressed can make queries faster because the target column does not need to be decompressed for lookup. Most implementations support data versioning while some support specifying an expiry time for column data. When the expiry time has passed, the data is automatically removed.

A column-family storage device is appropriate when:

- realtime random read/write capability is needed and data being stored has some defined structure

- data represents a tabular structure, each row consists of a large number of columns and nested groups of interrelated data exist

- support for schema evolution is required as column families can be added or removed without any system downtime

- certain fields are mostly accessed together, and searches need to be performed using field values

- efficient use of storage is required when the data consists of sparsely populated rows since column-family databases only allocate storage space if a column exists for a row. If no column is present, no space is allocated.

- query patterns involve insert, select, update and delete operations

A column-family storage device is inappropriate when:

- relational data access is required; for example, joins

- ACID transactional support is required

- binary data needs to be stored

- SQL-compliant queries need to be executed

- query patterns are likely to change frequently because that could initiate a corresponding restructuring of how column-families are arranged

Examples of column-family storage devices include Cassandra, HBase and Amazon SimpleDB.

Graph

Graph storage devices are used to persist inter-connected entities. Unlike other NoSQL storage devices, where the emphasis is on the structure of the entities, graph storage devices place emphasis on storing the linkages between entities (Figure 7.14).

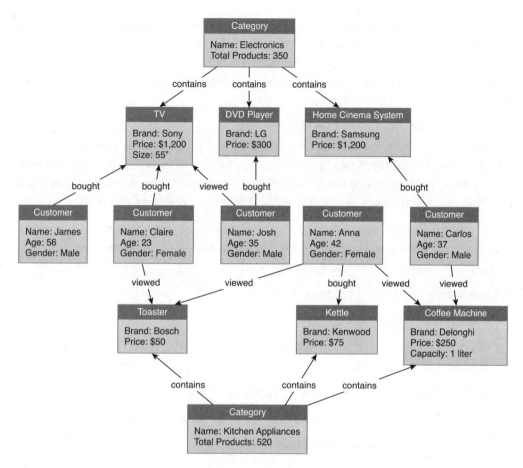

Figure 7.14
Graph storage devices store entities and their relationships.

Entities are stored as nodes (not to be confused with *cluster nodes*) and are also called vertices, while the linkages between entities are stored as edges. In RDBMS parlance, each node can be thought of a single row while the edge denotes a join.

Nodes can have more than one type of link between them through multiple edges. Each node can have attribute data as key-value pairs, such as a customer node with ID, name and age attributes.

Each edge can have its own attribute data as key-value pairs, which can be used to further filter query results. Having multiple edges are similar to defining multiple foreign keys in an RDBMS; however, not every node is required to have the same edges. Queries generally involve finding interconnected nodes based on node attributes and/or edge attributes, commonly referred to as node traversal. Edges can be unidirectional or bidirectional, setting the node traversal direction. Generally, graph storage devices provide consistency via ACID compliance.

The degree of usefulness of a graph storage device depends on the number and types of edges defined between the nodes. The greater the number and more diverse the edges are, the more diverse the types of queries it can handle. As a result, it is important to comprehensively capture the types of relations that exist between the nodes. This is not only true for existing usage scenarios, but also for exploratory analysis of data.

Graph storage devices generally allow adding new types of nodes without making changes to the database. This also enables defining additional links between nodes as new types of relationships or nodes appear in the database.

A graph storage device is appropriate when:

- interconnected entities need to be stored

- querying entities based on the type of relationship with each other rather than the attributes of the entities

- finding groups of interconnected entities

- finding distances between entities in terms of the node traversal distance

- mining data with a view toward finding patterns

A graph storage device is inappropriate when:

- updates are required to a large number of node attributes or edge attributes, as this involves searching for nodes or edges, which is a costly operation compared to performing node traversals

- entities have a large number of attributes or nested data—it is best to store light-weight entities in a graph storage device while storing the rest of the attribute data in a separate non-graph NoSQL storage device

- binary storage is required

- queries based on the selection of node/edge attributes dominate node traversal queries

Examples include Neo4J, Infinite Graph and OrientDB.

NewSQL Databases

NoSQL storage devices are highly scalable, available, fault-tolerant and fast for read/write operations. However, they do not provide the same transaction and consistency support as exhibited by ACID compliant RDBMSs. Following the BASE model, NoSQL storage devices provide eventual consistency rather than immediate consistency. They therefore will be in a soft state while reaching the state of eventual consistency. As a result, they are not appropriate for use when implementing large scale transactional systems.

NewSQL storage devices combine the ACID properties of RDBMS with the scalability and fault tolerance offered by NoSQL storage devices. NewSQL databases generally support SQL compliant syntax for data definition and data manipulation operations, and they often use a logical relational data model for data storage.

NewSQL databases can be used for developing OLTP systems with very high volumes of transactions, for example a banking system. They can also be used for realtime analytics, for example operational analytics, as some implementations leverage in-memory storage.

As compared to a NoSQL storage device, a NewSQL storage device provides an easier transition from a traditional RDBMS to a highly scalable database due to its support for SQL.

Examples of NewSQL databases include VoltDB, NuoDB and InnoDB.

In-Memory Storage Devices

The preceding section introduced the on-disk storage device and its various types as a fundamental means of data storage. This section builds upon this knowledge by presenting in-memory storage as a means of providing options for highly performant, advanced data storage.

An in-memory storage device generally utilizes RAM, the main memory of a computer, as its storage medium to provide fast data access. The growing capacity and decreasing cost of RAM, coupled with the increasing read/write speed of solid state hard drives, has made it possible to develop in-memory data storage solutions.

Storage of data in memory eliminates the latency of disk I/O and the data transfer time between the main memory and the hard drive. This overall reduction in data read/write latency makes data processing much faster. In-memory storage device capacity can be increased massively by horizontally scaling the cluster that is hosting the in-memory storage device.

Cluster-based memory enables storage of large amounts of data, including Big Data datasets, which can be accessed considerably faster when compared with an on-disk storage device. This significantly reduces the overall execution time of Big Data analytics, thus enabling realtime Big Data analytics.

Figure 7.15 shows the symbol that represents an in-memory storage device. Figure 7.16 illustrates an access time comparison between in-memory and on-disk storage devices. The top of the figure shows that a sequential read of 1 MB of data from an in-memory storage device takes around 0.25 ms. The bottom half of the figure shows that reading the same amount of data from an on-disk storage device takes around 20 ms. This demonstrates that reading data from in-memory storage is approximately 80 times faster than on-disk storage. Note that it is assumed that the network data transfer time is the same across the two scenarios and it has therefore been excluded from the read time.

in-memory
storage device

Figure 7.15

The symbol used to represent an in-memory storage device.

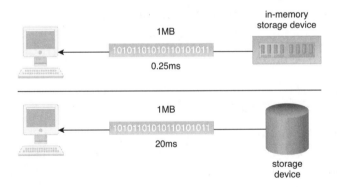

Figure 7.16

In-memory storage devices are 80 times faster at transferring data than on-disk storage devices.

An in-memory storage device enables in-memory analytics, which refers to in-memory analysis of data, such as generating statistics by executing queries on data that is stored in memory instead of on disk. In-memory analytics enable operational analytics and operational BI through fast execution of queries and algorithms.

Primarily, in-memory storage enables making sense of the fast influx of data in a Big Data environment (velocity characteristic) by providing a storage medium that facilitates realtime insight generation. This supports making quick business decisions for mitigating a threat or taking advantage of an opportunity.

A Big Data in-memory storage device is implemented over a cluster, providing high availability and redundancy. Therefore, horizontal scalability can be achieved by simply adding more nodes or memory. When compared with an on-disk storage device, an in-memory storage device is expensive because of the higher cost of memory as compared to a disk-based storage device.

Although a 64-bit machine can make use of 16 exabytes of memory, due to the physical limitations of the machine, such as the number of memory bays, the installed memory is considerably less. For scaling out, it is not just the addition of more memory, but also the addition of nodes that are required once the per node memory limit is reached. This increases the data storage cost.

Apart from being expensive, in-memory storage devices do not provide the same level of support for durable data storage. The price factor further affects the achievable capacity of an in-memory device when compared with an on-disk storage device. Consequently, only up-to-date and fresh data or data that has the most value is kept in memory, whereas stale data gets replaced with newer, fresher data.

Depending on how it is implemented, an in-memory storage device can support schema-less or schema-aware storage. Schema-less storage support is provided through key-value based data persistence.

An in-memory storage device is appropriate when:

- data arrives at a fast pace and requires realtime analytics or event stream processing

- continuous or always-on analytics is required, such as operational BI and operational analytics

- interactive query processing and realtime data visualization needs to be performed, including what-if analysis and drill-down operations

- the same dataset is required by multiple data processing jobs

- performing exploratory data analysis, as the same dataset does not need to be reloaded from disk if the algorithm changes

- data processing involves iterative access to the same dataset, such as executing graph-based algorithms

- developing low latency Big Data solutions with ACID transaction support

An in-memory storage device is inappropriate when:

- data processing consists of batch processing

- very large amounts of data need to be persisted in-memory for a long time in order to perform in-depth data analysis

- performing strategic BI or strategic analytics that involves access to very large amounts of data and involves batch data processing

- datasets are extremely large and do not fit into the available memory

- making the transition from traditional data analysis toward Big Data analysis, as incorporating an in-memory storage device may require additional skills and involves a complex setup

- an enterprise has a limited budget, as setting up an in-memory storage device may require upgrading nodes, which could either be done by node replacement or by adding more RAM

In-memory storage devices can be implemented as:

- In-Memory Data Grid (IMDG)

- In-Memory Database (IMDB)

Although both of these technologies use memory as their underlying data storage medium, what makes them distinct is the way data is stored in the memory. Key features of each of these technologies are discussed next.

In-Memory Data Grids

IMDGs store data in memory as key-value pairs across multiple nodes where the keys and values can be any business object or application data in serialized form. This supports schema-less data storage through storage of semi/unstructured data. Data access is typically provided via APIs. The symbol used to depict an IMDG is shown in Figure 7.17.

IMDG

Figure 7.17
The symbol used to represent an IMDG.

In Figure 7.18:

1. An image (a), XML data (b) and a customer object (c) are first serialized using a serialization engine.

2. They are then stored as key-value pairs in an IMDG.

3. A client requests the customer object via its key.

4. The value is then returned by the IMDG in serialized form.

5. The client then utilizes a serialization engine to deserialize the value to obtain the customer object...

6. ... in order to manipulate the customer object.

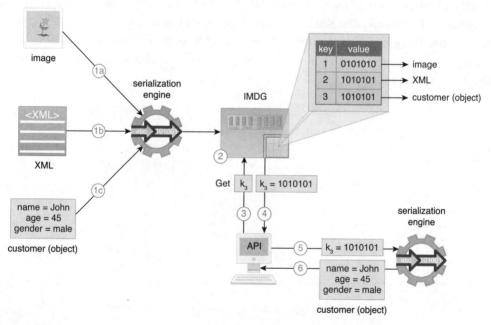

Figure 7.18
An IMDG storage device.

Nodes in IMDGs keep themselves synchronized and collectively provide high availability, fault tolerance and consistency. In comparison to NoSQL's eventual consistency approach, IMDGs support immediate consistency.

As compared to relational IMDBs (discussed under IMDB), IMDGs provide faster data access as IMDGs store non-relational data as objects. Hence, unlike relational IMDBs, object-to-relational mapping is not required and clients can work directly with the domain specific objects.

IMDGs scale horizontally by implementing data partitioning and data replication and further support reliability by replicating data to at least one extra node. In case of a machine failure, IMDGs automatically re-create lost copies of data from replicas as part of the recovery process.

IMDGs are heavily used for realtime analytics because they support Complex Event Processing (CEP) via the publish-subscribe messaging model. This is achieved through a feature called *continuous querying*, also known as active querying, where a filter for event(s) of interest is registered with the IMDG. The IMDG then continuously evaluates the filter and whenever the filter is satisfied as a result of insert/update/delete operations, subscribing clients are informed (Figure 7.19). Notifications are sent asynchronously as change events, such as *added*, *removed* and *updated* events, with information about key-value pairs, such as *old* and *new* values.

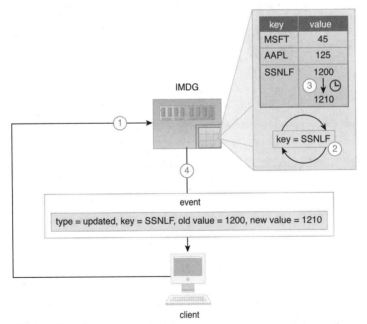

Figure 7.19
An IMDG stores stock prices where the key is the stock symbol, and the value is the stock price (shown as text for readability). A client issues a continuous query (key=SSNLF) (1) which is registered in the IMDG (2). When the stock price for SSNLF stock changes (3), an updated event is sent to the subscribing client that contains various details about the event (4).

From a functionality point of view, an IMDG is akin to a distributed cache as both provide memory-based access to frequently accessed data. However, unlike a distributed cache, an IMDG provides built in support for replication and high availability.

Realtime processing engines can make use of IMDG where high velocity data is stored in the IMDG as it arrives and is processed there before being saved to an on-disk storage device, or data from the on-disk storage device is copied to the IMDG. This makes data processing orders of magnitude faster and further enables data-reuse in case multiple jobs or iterative algorithms are run against the same data. IMDGs may also support in-memory MapReduce that helps to reduce the latency of disk based MapReduce processing, especially when the same job needs to be executed multiple times.

An IMDG can also be deployed within a cloud based environment where it provides a flexible storage medium that can scale out or scale in automatically as the storage demand increases or decreases, as shown in Figure 7.20.

IMDGs can be added to existing Big Data solutions by introducing them between the existing on-disk storage device and the data processing application. However, this introduction generally requires changing the application code to implement the IMDGs API.

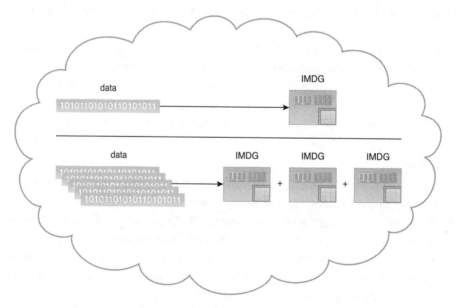

Figure 7.20
An IMDG deployed in a cloud scales out automatically as the demand for data storage increases.

Note that some IMDG implementations may also provide limited or full SQL support.

Examples include In-Memory Data Fabric, Hazelcast and Oracle Coherence.

In a Big Data solution environment, IMDGs are often deployed together with on-disk storage devices that act as the backend storage. This is achieved via the following approaches that can be combined as necessary to support read/write performance, consistency and simplicity requirements:

- read-through
- write-through
- write-behind
- refresh-ahead

Read-through

If a requested value for a key is not found in the IMDG, then it is synchronously read from the backend on-disk storage device, such as a database. Upon a successful read from the backend on-disk storage device, the key-value pair is inserted into the IMDG, and the requested value is returned to the client. Any subsequent requests for the same key are then served by the IMDG directly, instead of the backend storage. Although it is a simple approach, its synchronous nature may introduce read latency. Figure 7.21 is an example of the read-through approach, where Client A tries to read key K3 (1) which does not currently exist in the IMDG. Consequently, it is read from the backend storage (2) and inserted into the IMDG (3) before being sent to Client A (4). A subsequent request for the same key by Client B (5) is then served directly by the IMDG (6).

Write-through

Any write (insert/update/delete) to the IMDG is written synchronously in a transactional manner to the backend on-disk storage device, such as a database. If the write to the backend on-disk storage device fails, the IMDG's update is rolled back. Due to this transactional nature, data consistency is achieved immediately between the two data stores. However, this transactional support is provided at the expense of write latency as any write operation is considered complete only when feedback (write success/failure) from the backend storage is received (Figure 7.22).

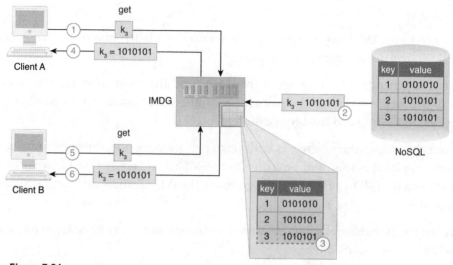

Figure 7.21

An example of using an IMDG with the read-through approach.

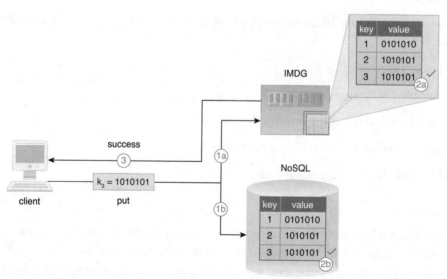

Figure 7.22

A client inserts a new key-value pair (K3,V3) which is inserted into both the IMDG (1a) and the backend storage (1b) in a transactional manner. Upon successful insertion of data into the IMDG (2a) and the backend storage (2b), the client is informed that data has been successfully inserted (3).

Write-behind

Any write to the IMDG is written asynchronously in a batch manner to the backend on-disk storage device, such as a database.

A queue is generally placed between the IMDG and the backend storage for keeping track of the required changes to the backend storage. This queue can be configured to write data to the backend storage at different intervals.

The asynchronous nature increases both write performance (the write operation is considered completed as soon as it is written to the IMDG) and read performance (data can be read from the IMDG as soon as it is written to the IMDG) and scalability/availability in general.

However, the asynchronous nature introduces inconsistency until the backend storage is updated at the specified interval.

In Figure 7.23:

1. Client A updates value of K3, which is updated in the IMDG (a) and is also sent to a queue (b).

2. However, before the backend storage is updated, Client B makes a request for the same key.

3. The old value is sent.

4. After the configured interval…

5. … the backend storage is eventually updated.

6. Client C makes a request for the same key.

7. This time, the updated value is sent.

Refresh-ahead

Refresh-ahead is a proactive approach where any frequently accessed values are automatically, asynchronously refreshed in the IMDG, provided that the value is accessed before its expiry time as configured in the IMDG. If a value is accessed after its expiry time, the value, like in the read-through approach, is synchronously read from the backend storage and updated in the IMDG before being returned to the client.

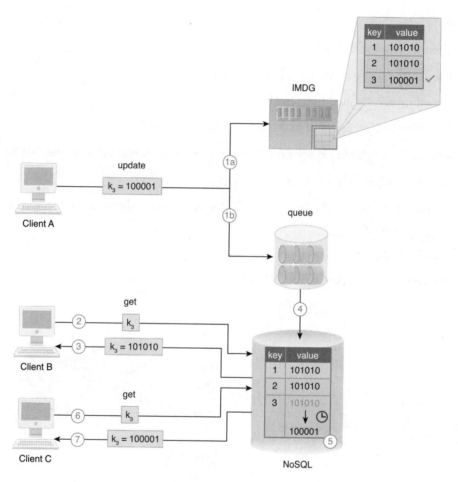

Figure 7.23
An example of the write-behind approach.

Due to its asynchronous and forward-looking nature, this approach helps achieve better read-performance and is especially useful when the same values are accessed frequently or accessed by a number of clients.

Compared to the read-through approach, where a value is served from the IMDG until its expiry, data inconsistency between the IMDG and the backend storage is minimized as values are refreshed before they expire.

In Figure 7.24:

1. Client A requests K3 before its expiry time.

2. The current value is returned from the IMDG.

3. The value is refreshed from the backend storage.

4. The value is then updated in the IMDG asynchronously.

5. After the configured expiry time, the key-value pair is evicted from the IMDG.

6. Now Client B makes a request for K3.

7. As the key does not exist in the IMDG, it is synchronously requested from the backend storage...

8. ...and updated.

9. The value is then returned to Client B.

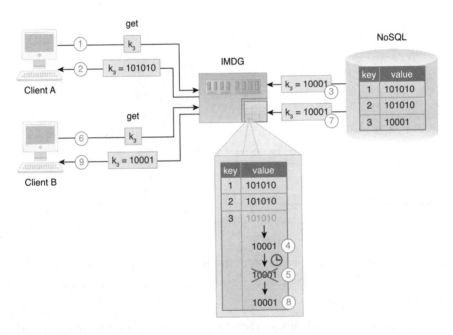

Figure 7.24
An example of an IMDG leveraging the refresh-ahead approach.

An IMDG storage device is appropriate when:

- data needs to be readily accessible in object form with minimal latency

- data being stored is non-relational in nature such as semi-structured and unstructured data

- adding realtime support to an existing Big Data solution currently using on-disk storage

- the existing storage device cannot be replaced but the data access layer can be modified

- scalability is more important than relational storage; although IMDGs are more scalable than IMDBs (IMDBs are functionally complete databases), they do not support relational storage

Examples of IMDG storage devices include: Hazelcast, Infinispan, Pivotal GemFire and Gigaspaces XAP.

In-Memory Databases

IMDBs are in-memory storage devices that employ database technology and leverage the performance of RAM to overcome runtime latency issues that plague on-disk storage devices. The symbol for an IMDB is shown in Figure 7.25.

IMDB

Figure 7.25
The symbol used to represent an IMDB.

In Figure 7.26:

1. A relational dataset is stored into an IMDB.

2. A client requests a customer record (id = 2) via SQL.

3. The relevant customer record is then returned by the IMDB, which is directly manipulated by the client without the need for any deserialization.

An IMDB can be relational in nature (relational IMDB) for the storage of structured data, or may leverage NoSQL technology (non-relational IMDB) for the storage of semi-structured and unstructured data.

Unlike IMDGs, which generally provide data access via APIs, relational IMDBs make use of the more familiar SQL language, which helps data analysts or data scientists that do not have advanced programming skills. NoSQL-based IMDBs generally provide

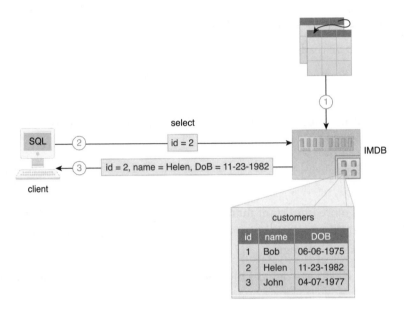

Figure 7.26
An example depicting the retrieval of data from an IMDB.

API-based access, which may be as simple as put, get and delete operations. Depending on the underlying implementation, some IMDBs scale-out, while others scale-up, to achieve scalability.

Not all IMDB implementations directly support durability, but instead leverage various strategies for providing durability in the face of machine failures or memory corruption. These strategies include the following:

- Use of Non-volatile RAM (NVRAM) for storing data permanently.

- Database transaction logs can be periodically stored to a non-volatile medium, such as disk.

- Snapshot files, which capture database state at a certain point in time, are saved to disk.

- An IMDB may leverage sharding and replication to support increasing availability and reliability as a substitute for durability.

- IMDBs can be used in conjunction with on-disk storage devices such as NoSQL databases and RDBMSs for durable storage.

Like an IMDG, an IMDB may also support the continuous query feature, where a filter in the form of a query for data of interest is registered with the IMDB. The IMDB then continuously executes the query in an iterative manner. Whenever the query result is modified as a result of insert/update/delete operations, subscribing clients are asynchronously informed by sending out changes as events, such as *added*, *removed* and *updated* events, with information about record values, such as *old* and *new* values.

In Figure 7.27, an IMDB stores temperature values for various sensors. The following steps are shown:

1. A client issues a continuous query (select * from sensors where temperature > 75).

2. It is registered in the IMDB.

3. When the temperature for any sensor exceeds 75F ...

4. ... an updated event is sent to the subscribing client that contains various details about the event.

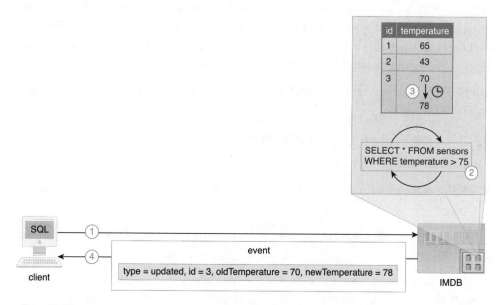

Figure 7.27
An example of IMDB storage configured with a continuous query.

IMDBs are heavily used in realtime analytics and can further be used for developing low latency applications requiring full ACID transaction support (relational IMDB). In comparison with IMDGs, IMDBs provide an easy to set up in-memory data storage option, as IMDBs do not generally require on-disk backend storage devices.

Introduction of IMDBs into an existing Big Data solution generally requires replacement of existing on-disk storage devices, including any RDBMSs if used. In the case of replacing an RDBMS with a relational IMDB, little or no application code change is required due to SQL support provided by the relational IMDB. However, when replacing an RDBMS with a NoSQL IMDB, code change may be required due to the need to implement the IMDB's NoSQL APIs.

In the case of replacing an on-disk NoSQL database with a relational IMDB, code change will often be required to establish SQL-based access. However, when replacing an on-disk NoSQL database with a NoSQL IMDB, code change may still be required due to the implementation of new APIs.

Relational IMDBs are generally less scalable than IMDGs, as relational IMDBs need to support distributed queries and transactions across the cluster. Some IMDB implementations may benefit from scaling up, which helps to address the latency that occurs when executing queries and transactions in a scale-out environment.

Examples include Aerospike, MemSQL, Altibase HDB, eXtreme DB and Pivotal GemFire XD.

An IMDB storage device is appropriate when:

- relational data needs to be stored in memory with ACID support
- adding realtime support to an existing Big Data solution currently using on-disk storage
- the existing on-disk storage device can be replaced with an in-memory equivalent technology
- it is required to minimize changes to the data access layer of the application code, such as when the application consists of an SQL-based data access layer
- relational storage is more important than scalability

CASE STUDY EXAMPLE

ETI's IT team is evaluating the use of different Big Data storage technologies for storing the range of datasets identified in Chapter 1. Following the data processing strategy, the team decides to introduce on-disk storage technologies to enable batch processing of data and to incorporate in-memory storage technologies that support realtime data processing. The team identifies that it needs to utilize a combination of the distributed file system and NoSQL databases to store a variety of raw datasets produced both within and beyond ETI's boundaries and to store processed data.

Any line-based textual dataset, such as webserver log files, where a record is represented by a delimited line of text and the dataset can be processed in a streaming fashion (records are processed one after the other without requiring random access to specific records), will be stored in Hadoop's distributed file system (HDFS).

The incident photographs have a large storage footprint and are currently stored in a relational database as a BLOB with an *ID* that corresponds to the *incident ID*. Since these photographs are binary data and need to be accessed via their *IDs*, the IT team believes that a key-value database can be used instead to store them. This will provide an inexpensive means of storing incident photographs and will free up space on the relational database.

A NoSQL document database will be used to store hierarchical data that includes Twitter data (JSON), weather data (XML), call center agent notes (XML), claim adjuster notes (XML), health records (HL7 compliant records in XML) and emails (XML).

When a natural grouping of fields exists and related fields are accessed together, data is saved in a NoSQL column-family database. For example, the customer profile data consists of customer's personal details, address and interests as well as current policy fields that each consist of multiple fields. On the other hand, processed tweets and weather data can also be stored in a column-family database since the processed data needs to be in a tabular form from which individual fields can be accessed for different analytical queries.

Chapter 8

Big Data Analysis Techniques

Quantitative Analysis

Qualitative Analysis

Data Mining

Statistical Analysis

Machine Learning

Semantic Analysis

Visual Analysis

Big Data analysis blends traditional statistical data analysis approaches with computational ones. Statistical sampling from a population is ideal when the entire dataset is available, and this condition is typical of traditional batch processing scenarios. However, Big Data can shift batch processing to realtime processing due to the need to make sense of streaming data. With streaming data, the dataset accumulates over time, and the data is time-ordered. Streaming data places an emphasis on timely processing, for analytic results have a shelf-life. Whether it is the recognition of an upsell opportunity that presents itself due to the current context of a customer, or the detection of anomalous conditions in an industrial setting that require intervention to protect equipment or ensure product quality, time is of the essence, and freshness of the analytic result is essential.

In any fast moving field like Big Data, there are always opportunities for innovation. An example of this is the question of how to best blend statistical and computational approaches for a given analytical problem. Statistical techniques are commonly preferred for exploratory data analysis, after which computational techniques that leverage the insight gleaned from the statistical study of a dataset can be applied. The shift from batch to realtime presents other challenges as realtime techniques need to leverage computationally-efficient algorithms.

In 2003, William Agresti recognized the shift toward computational approaches and argued for the creation of a new computational discipline named Discovery Informatics. Agresti's view of this field was one that embraced composition. In other words, he believed that discovery informatics was a synthesis of the following fields: pattern recognition (data mining); artificial intelligence (machine learning); document and text processing (semantic processing); database management and information storage and retrieval. Agresti's insight into the importance and breadth of computational approaches to data analysis was forward-thinking at the time, and his perspective on the matter has only been reinforced by the passage of time and the emergence of data science as a discipline.

One challenge concerns the best way of balancing the accuracy of an analytic result against the run-time of the algorithm. In many cases, an approximation may be sufficient and affordable. From a storage perspective, multi-tiered storage solutions which leverage RAM, solid-state drives and hard-disk drives will provide near-term flexibility and realtime analytic capability with long-term, cost-effective persistent storage. In the long run, an organization will operate its Big Data analysis engine at two speeds: processing streaming data as it arrives and performing batch analysis of this data as it accumulates to look for patterns and trends. (The symbol used to represent data analysis is shown in Figure 8.1.)

Figure 8.1

The symbol used to represent data analysis.

This chapter begins with descriptions of the following basic types of data analysis:

- quantitative analysis
- qualitative analysis
- data mining
- statistical analysis
- machine learning
- semantic analysis
- visual analysis

Quantitative Analysis

Quantitative analysis is a data analysis technique that focuses on quantifying the patterns and correlations found in the data. Based on statistical practices, this technique involves analyzing a large number of observations from a dataset. Since the sample size is large, the results can be applied in a generalized manner to the entire dataset. Figure 8.2 depicts the fact that quantitative analysis produces numerical results.

Quantitative analysis results are absolute in nature and can therefore be used for numerical comparisons. For example, a quantitative analysis of ice cream sales may discover that a 5 degree increase in temperature increases ice cream sales by 15%.

Figure 8.2

The output of quantitative analysis is numerical in nature.

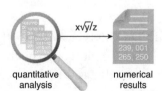

quantitative analysis

$x\sqrt{y}/z$

numerical results

Qualitative Analysis

Qualitative analysis is a data analysis technique that focuses on describing various data qualities using words. It involves analyzing a smaller sample in greater depth compared to quantitative data analysis. These analysis results cannot be generalized to an entire dataset due to the small sample size. They also cannot be measured numerically or used for numerical comparisons. For example, an analysis of ice cream sales may reveal that May's sales figures were not as high as June's. The analysis results state only that the figures were "not as high as," and do not provide a numerical difference. The output of qualitative analysis is a description of the relationship using words as shown in Figure 8.3.

Figure 8.3
Qualitative results are descriptive in nature and not generalizable to the entire dataset.

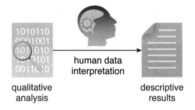

qualitative
analysis

human data
interpretation

descriptive
results

Data Mining

Data mining, also known as data discovery, is a specialized form of data analysis that targets large datasets. In relation to Big Data analysis, data mining generally refers to automated, software-based techniques that sift through massive datasets to identify patterns and trends.

Figure 8.4
The symbol used to represent data mining.

Specifically, it involves extracting hidden or unknown patterns in the data with the intention of identifying previously unknown patterns. Data mining forms the basis for predictive analytics and business intelligence (BI). The symbol used to represent data mining is shown in Figure 8.4.

Statistical Analysis

Statistical analysis uses statistical methods based on mathematical formulas as a means for analyzing data. Statistical analysis is most often quantitative, but can also be qualitative. This type of analysis is commonly used to describe datasets via summarization, such as providing the mean, median, or mode of statistics associated with the dataset. It can also be used to infer patterns and relationships within the dataset, such as regression and correlation.

This section describes the following types of statistical analysis:

- A/B Testing

- Correlation

- Regression

A/B Testing

A/B testing, also known as split or bucket testing, compares two versions of an element to determine which version is superior based on a pre-defined metric. The element can be a range of things. For example, it can be content, such as a Web page, or an offer for a product or service, such as deals on electronic items. The current version of the element is called the control version, whereas the modified version is called the treatment. Both versions are subjected to an experiment simultaneously. The observations are recorded to determine which version is more successful.

Although A/B testing can be implemented in almost any domain, it is most often used in marketing. Generally, the objective is to gauge human behavior with the goal of increasing sales. For example, in order to determine the best possible layout for an ice cream ad on Company A's Web site, two different versions of the ad are used. Version A is an existing ad (the control) while Version B has had its layout slightly altered (the treatment). Both versions are then simultaneously shown to different users:

- Version A to Group A

- Version B to Group B

The analysis of the results reveals that Version B of the ad resulted in more sales as compared to Version A.

In other areas such as the scientific domains, the objective may simply be to observe which version works better in order to improve a process or product. Figure 8.5 provides an example of A/B testing on two different email versions sent simultaneously.

Sample questions can include:

- *Is the new version of a drug better than the old one?*

- *Do customers respond better to advertisements delivered by email or postal mail?*

- *Is the newly designed homepage of the Web site generating more user traffic?*

Email A   Email B

Figure 8.5

Two different email versions are sent out simultaneously as part of a marketing campaign to see which version brings in more prospective customers.

Correlation

Correlation is an analysis technique used to determine whether two variables are related to each other. If they are found to be related, the next step is to determine what their relationship is. For example, the value of Variable A increases whenever the value of Variable B increases. We may be further interested in discovering how closely Variables A and B are related, which means we may also want to analyze the extent to which Variable B increases in relation to Variable A's increase.

The use of correlation helps to develop an understanding of a dataset and find relationships that can assist in explaining a phenomenon. Correlation is therefore commonly used for data mining where the identification of relationships between variables in a dataset leads to the discovery of patterns and anomalies. This can reveal the nature of the dataset or the cause of a phenomenon.

When two variables are considered to be correlated they are aligned based on a linear relationship. This means that when one variable changes, the other variable also changes proportionally and constantly.

Correlation is expressed as a decimal number between –1 to +1, which is known as the correlation coefficient. The degree of relationship changes from being strong to weak when moving from –1 to 0 or +1 to 0.

Figure 8.6 shows a correlation of +1, which suggests that there is a strong positive relationship between the two variables.

Figure 8.7 shows a correlation of 0, which suggests that there is no relationship at all between the two variables.

In Figure 8.8, a slope of –1 suggests that there is a strong negative relationship between the two variables.

Figure 8.6
When one variable increases,
the other also increases and
vice versa.

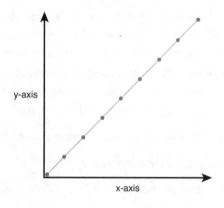

Figure 8.7
When one variable increases,
the other may stay the same, or
increase or decrease arbitrarily.

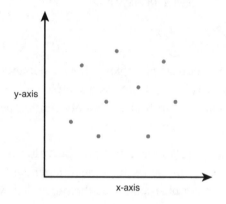

Figure 8.8
When one variable increases,
the other decreases and vice
versa.

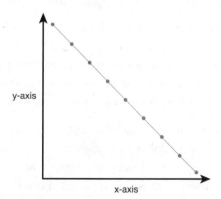

For example, managers believe that ice cream stores need to stock more ice cream for hot days, but don't know how much extra to stock. To determine if a relationship actually exists between temperature and ice cream sales, the analysts first apply correlation to the number of ice creams sold and the recorded temperature readings. A value of +0.75 suggests that there exists a strong relationship between the two. This relationship indicates that as temperature increases, more ice creams are sold.

Further sample questions addressed by correlation can include:

- *Does distance from the sea affect the temperature of a city?*

- *Do students who perform well at elementary school perform equally well at high school?*

- *To what extent is obesity linked with overeating?*

Regression

The analysis technique of regression explores how a dependent variable is related to an independent variable within a dataset. As a sample scenario, regression could help determine the type of relationship that exists between temperature, the independent variable, and crop yield, the dependent variable.

Applying this technique helps determine how the value of the dependent variable changes in relation to changes in the value of the independent variable. When the independent variable increases, for example, does the dependent variable also increase? If yes, is the increase in a linear or non-linear proportion?

For example, in order to determine how much extra stock each ice cream store needs to have, the analysts apply regression by feeding in the values of temperature readings. These values are based on the weather forecast as an independent variable and the number of ice creams sold as the dependent variable. What the analysts discover is that 15% of additional stock is required for every 5-degree increase in temperature.

More than one independent variable can be tested at the same time. However, in such cases, only one independent variable may change, while others are kept constant. Regression can help enable a better understanding of what a phenomenon is and why it occurred. It can also be used to make predictions about the values of the dependent variable.

Linear regression represents a constant rate of change, as shown in Figure 8.9.

Non-linear regression represents a variable rate of change, as shown in Figure 8.10.

Figure 8.9
Linear regression

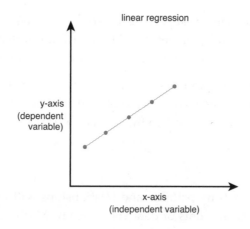

Figure 8.10
Non-linear regression

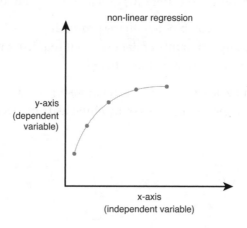

Sample questions can include:

- *What will be the temperature of a city that is 250 miles away from the sea?*

- *What will be the grades of a student studying at a high school based on their primary school grades?*

- *What are the chances that a person will be obese based on the amount of their food intake?*

Regression and correlation have a number of important differences. Correlation does not imply causation. The change in the value of one variable may not be responsible for the change in the value of the second variable, although both may change at the same rate. This can occur due to an unknown third variable, known as the confounding factor. Correlation assumes that both variables are independent.

Regression, on the other hand, is applicable to variables that have previously been identified as dependent and independent variables and implies that there is a degree of causation between the variables. The causation may be direct or indirect.

Within Big Data, correlation can first be applied to discover if a relationship exists. Regression can then be applied to further explore the relationship and predict the values of the dependent variable, based on the known values of the independent variable.

Machine Learning

Humans are good at spotting patterns and relationships within data. Unfortunately, we cannot process large amounts of data very quickly. Machines, on the other hand, are very adept at processing large amounts of data quickly, but only if they know how.

If human knowledge can be combined with the processing speed of machines, machines will be able to process large amounts of data without requiring much human intervention. This is the basic concept of machine learning.

In this section, machine learning and its relationship to data mining are explored through coverage of the following types of machine learning techniques:

- Classification
- Clustering
- Outlier Detection
- Filtering

Classification (Supervised Machine Learning)

Classification is a supervised learning technique by which data is classified into relevant, previously learned categories. It consists of two steps:

1. The system is fed training data that is already categorized or labeled, so that it can develop an understanding of the different categories.

2. The system is fed unknown but similar data for classification and based on the understanding it developed from the training data, the algorithm will classify the unlabeled data.

A common application of this technique is for the filtering of email spam. Note that classification can be performed for two or more categories. In a simplified classification process, the machine is fed labeled data during training that builds its understanding of the classification, as shown in Figure 8.11. The machine is then fed unlabeled data, which it classifies itself.

Figure 8.11

Machine learning can be used to automatically classify datasets.

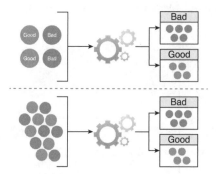

For example, a bank wants to find out which of its customers is likely to default on loan payments. Based on historic data, a training dataset is compiled that contains labeled examples of customers that have or have not previously defaulted. This training data is fed to a classification algorithm that is used to develop an understanding of "good" and "bad" customers. Finally, new untagged customer data is fed in order to find out whether a given customer belongs to the defaulting category.

Sample questions can include:

- *Should an applicant's credit card application be accepted or rejected based on other accepted or rejected applications?*

- *Is a tomato a fruit or a vegetable based on the known examples of fruit and vegetables?*

- *Do the medical test results for the patient indicate a risk for a heart attack?*

Clustering (Unsupervised Machine Learning)

Clustering is an unsupervised learning technique by which data is divided into different groups so that the data in each group has similar properties. There is no prior learning of categories required. Instead, categories are implicitly generated based on the data groupings. How the data is grouped depends on the type of algorithm used. Each algorithm uses a different technique to identify clusters.

Clustering is generally used in data mining to get an understanding of the properties of a given dataset. After developing this understanding, classification can be used to make better predictions about similar but new or unseen data.

Clustering can be applied to the categorization of unknown documents and to personalized marketing campaigns by grouping together customers with similar behavior. A scatter graph provides a visual representation of clusters in Figure 8.12.

Figure 8.12

A scatter graph summarizes the results of clustering.

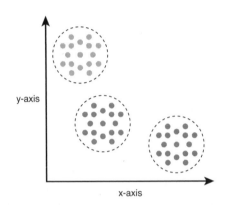

For example, a bank wants to introduce its existing customers to a range of new financial products based on the customer profiles it has on record. The analysts categorize customers into multiple groups using clustering. Each group is then introduced to one or more financial products most suitable to the characteristics of the overall profile of the group.

Sample questions can include:

- *How many different species of trees exist based on the similarity between trees?*

- *How many groups of customers exist based upon similar purchase history?*

- *What are the different groups of viruses based on their characteristics?*

Outlier Detection

Outlier detection is the process of finding data that is significantly different from or inconsistent with the rest of the data within a given dataset. This machine learning technique is used to identify anomalies, abnormalities and deviations that can be advantageous, such as opportunities, or unfavorable, such as risks.

Outlier detection is closely related to the concept of classification and clustering, although its algorithms focus on finding abnormal values. It can be based on either supervised or unsupervised learning. Applications for outlier detection include fraud detection, medical diagnosis, network data analysis and sensor data analysis. A scatter graph visually highlights data points that are outliers, as shown in Figure 8.13.

Figure 8.13
A scatter graph highlights
an outlier.

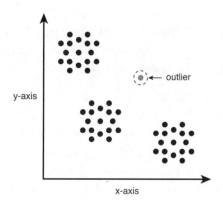

For example, in order to find out whether or not a transaction is likely to be fraudulent, the bank's IT team builds a system employing an outlier detection technique that is based on supervised learning. A set of known fraudulent transactions is first fed into the outlier detection algorithm. After training the system, unknown transactions are then fed into the outlier detection algorithm to predict if they are fraudulent or not.

Sample questions can include:

- *Is an athlete using performance enhancing drugs?*

- *Are there any wrongly identified fruits and vegetables in the training dataset used for a classification task?*

- *Is there a particular strain of virus that does not respond to medication?*

Filtering

Filtering is the automated process of finding relevant items from a pool of items. Items can be filtered either based on a user's own behavior or by matching the behavior of multiple users. Filtering is generally applied via the following two approaches:

- collaborative filtering

- content-based filtering

A common medium by which filtering is implemented is via the use of a recommender system. Collaborative filtering is an item filtering technique based on the collaboration, or merging, of a user's past behavior with the behaviors of others. A target user's past behavior, including their likes, ratings, purchase history and more, is collaborated with the behavior of similar users. Based on the similarity of the users' behavior, items are filtered for the target user.

Collaborative filtering is solely based on the similarity between users' behavior. It requires a large amount of user behavior data in order to accurately filter items. It is an example of the application of the law of large numbers.

Content-based filtering is an item filtering technique focused on the similarity between users and items. A user profile is created based on that user's past behavior, for example, their likes, ratings and purchase history. The similarities identified between the user profile and the attributes of various items lead to items being filtered for the user. Contrary to collaborative filtering, content-based filtering is solely dedicated to individual user preferences and does not require data about other users.

A recommender system predicts user preferences and generates suggestions for the user accordingly. Suggestions commonly pertain to recommending items, such as movies, books, Web pages and people. A recommender system typically uses either collaborative filtering or content-based filtering to generate suggestions. It may also be based on a hybrid of both collaborative filtering and content-based filtering to fine-tune the accuracy and effectiveness of generated suggestions.

For example, in order to realize cross-selling opportunities, the bank builds a recommender system that uses content-based filtering. Based on matches found between financial products purchased by customers and the properties of similar financial products, the recommender system automates suggestions for potential financial products that customers may also be interested in.

Sample questions can include:

- *How can only the news articles that a user is interested in be displayed?*

- *Which holiday destinations can be recommended based on the travel history of a vacationer?*

- *Which other new users can be suggested as friends based on the current profile of a person?*

Semantic Analysis

A fragment of text or speech data can carry different meanings in different contexts, whereas a complete sentence may retain its meaning, even if structured in different ways. In order for the machines to extract valuable information, text and speech data needs to be understood by the machines in the same way as humans do. Semantic analysis represents practices for extracting meaningful information from textual and speech data.

This section describes the following types of semantic analysis:

- Natural Language Processing

- Text Analytics

- Sentiment Analysis

Natural Language Processing

Natural language processing is a computer's ability to comprehend human speech and text as naturally understood by humans. This allows computers to perform a variety of useful tasks, such as full-text searches.

For example, in order to increase the quality of customer care, the ice cream company employs natural language processing to transcribe customer calls into textual data that are then mined for commonly recurring reasons of customer dissatisfaction.

Instead of hard-coding the required learning rules, either supervised or unsupervised machine learning is applied to develop the computer's understanding of the natural language. In general, the more learning data the computer has, the more correctly it can decipher human text and speech.

Natural language processing includes both text and speech recognition. For speech recognition, the system attempts to comprehend the speech and then performs an action, such as transcribing text.

Sample questions can include:

- *How can an automated phone exchange system that can recognize the correct department extension as dictated verbally by the caller be developed?*

- *How can grammatical mistakes be automatically identified?*

- *How can a system that can correctly understand different accents of English language be designed?*

Text Analytics

Unstructured text is generally much more difficult to analyze and search in comparison to structured text. Text analytics is the specialized analysis of text through the application of data mining, machine learning and natural language processing techniques to extract value out of unstructured text. Text analytics essentially provides the ability to discover text rather than just search it.

Useful insights from text-based data can be gained by helping businesses develop an understanding of the information that is contained within a large body of text. As a continuation of the preceding NLP example, the transcribed textual data is further analyzed using text analytics to extract meaningful information about the common reasons behind customer discontent.

The basic tenet of text analytics is to turn unstructured text into data that can be searched and analyzed. As the amount of digitized documents, emails, social media posts and log files increases, businesses have an increasing need to leverage any value that can be extracted from these forms of semi-structured and unstructured data. Solely analyzing operational (structured) data may cause businesses to miss out on cost-saving or business expansion opportunities, especially those that are customer-focused.

Applications include document classification and search, as well as building a 360-degree view of a customer by extracting information from a CRM system.

Text analytics generally involves two steps:

1. Parsing text within documents to extract:

    • Named Entities – person, group, place, company

    • Pattern-Based Entities – social security number, zip code

    • Concepts – an abstract representation of an entity

    • Facts – relationship between entities

2. Categorization of documents using these extracted entities and facts.

The extracted information can be used to perform a context-specific search on entities, based on the type of relationship that exists between the entities. Figure 8.14 shows a simplified representation of text analysis.

documents

Figure 8.14
Entities are extracted from text files using semantic rules and structured so that they can be searched.

Sample questions can include:

- *How can I categorize Web sites based on the content of their Web pages?*

- *How can I find the books that contain content that is relevant to the topic that I am studying?*

- *How can I identify contracts that contain confidential company information?*

Sentiment Analysis

Sentiment analysis is a specialized form of text analysis that focuses on determining the bias or emotions of individuals. This form of analysis determines the attitude of the author of the text by analyzing the text within the context of the natural language. Sentiment analysis not only provides information about how individuals feel, but also the intensity of their feeling. This information can then be integrated into the decision-making process. Common applications for sentiment analysis include identifying customer satisfaction or dissatisfaction early, gauging product success or failure, and spotting new trends.

For example, an ice cream company would like to learn about which of its ice cream flavors are most liked by children. Sales data alone does not provide this information because the children that consume the ice cream are not necessarily the purchasers of the ice cream. Sentiment analysis is applied to archived customer feedback left on the ice cream company's Web site to extract information specifically regarding children's preferences for certain ice cream flavors over other flavors.

Sample questions can include:

- *How can customer reactions to the new packaging of the product be gauged?*

- *Which contestant is a likely winner of a singing contest?*

- *Can customer churn be measured by social media comments?*

Visual Analysis

Visual analysis is a form of data analysis that involves the graphic representation of data to enable or enhance its visual perception. Based on the premise that humans can understand and draw conclusions from graphics more quickly than from text, visual analysis acts as a discovery tool in the field of Big Data.

The objective is to use graphic representations to develop a deeper understanding of the data being analyzed. Specifically, it helps identify and highlight hidden patterns, correlations and anomalies. Visual analysis is also directly related to exploratory data analysis as it encourages the formulation of questions from different angles.

This section describes the following types of visual analysis:

- Heat Maps
- Time Series Plots
- Network Graphs
- Spatial Data Mapping

Heat Maps

Heat maps are an effective visual analysis technique for expressing patterns, data compositions via part-whole relations and geographic distributions of data. They also facilitate the identification of areas of interest and the discovery of extreme (high/low) values within a dataset.

For example, in order to identify the top- and worst-selling regions for ice cream sales, the ice cream sales data is plotted using a heat map. Green is used to highlight the best performing regions, while red is used to highlight worst performing regions.

The heat map itself is a visual, color-coded representation of data values. Each value is given a color according to its type or the range that it falls under. For example, a heat map may assign the values of 0–3 to the color red, 4–6 to amber and 7–10 to green.

A heat map can be in the form of a chart or a map. A chart represents a matrix of values in which each cell is color-coded according to the value, as shown in Figure 8.15. It can also represent hierarchical values by using color-coded nested rectangles.

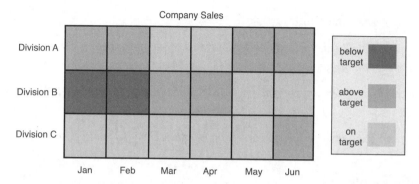

Figure 8.15

This chart heat map depicts the sales of three divisions within a company over a period of six months.

In Figure 8.16, a map represents a geographic measure by which different regions are color-coded or shaded according to a certain theme. Instead of coloring or shading the whole region, the map may be superimposed by a layer made up of collections of colored/shaded points relating to various regions, or colored/shaded shapes representing various regions.

Figure 8.16

A heat map of the US sales figures from 2013.

Sample questions can include:

- *How can I visually identify any patterns related to carbon emissions across a large number of cities around the world?*

- *How can I see if there are any patterns of different types of cancers in relation to different ethnicities?*

- *How can I analyze soccer players according to their strengths and weaknesses?*

Time Series Plots

Time series plots allow the analysis of data that is recorded over periodic intervals of time. This type of analysis makes use of time series, which is a time-ordered collection of values recorded over regular time intervals. An example is a time series that contains sales figures that are recorded at the end of each month.

Time series analysis helps to uncover patterns within data that are time-dependent. Once identified, the pattern can be extrapolated for future predictions. For example, to identify seasonal sales patterns, monthly ice cream sales figures are plotted as a time series, which further helps to forecast sales figures for the next season.

Time series analyses are usually used for forecasting by identifying long-term trends, seasonal periodic patterns and irregular short-term variations in the dataset. Unlike other types of analyses, time series analysis always includes time as a comparison variable, and the data collected is always time-dependent.

A time series plot is generally expressed using a line chart, with time plotted on the x-axis and the recorded data value plotted on the y-axis, as shown in Figure 8.17.

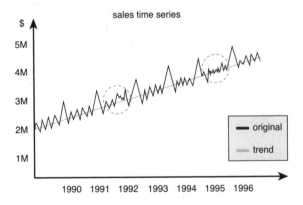

Figure 8.17
A line chart depicts a sales time series from 1990 to 1996.

The time series presented in Figure 8.17 spans seven years. The evenly spaced peaks toward the end of each year show seasonal periodic patterns, for example Christmas sales. The dotted red circles represent short-term irregular variations. The blue line shows an upward trend, indicating an increase in sales.

Sample questions can include:

- *How much yield should the farmer expect based on historical yield data?*

- *What is the expected increase in population in the next 5 years?*

- *Is the current decrease in sales a one-off occurrence or does it occur regularly?*

Network Graphs

Within the context of visual analysis, a network graph depicts an interconnected collection of entities. An entity can be a person, a group, or some other business domain object such as a product. Entities may be connected with one another directly or indirectly. Some connections may only be one-way, so that traversal in the reverse direction is not possible.

Network analysis is a technique that focuses on analyzing relationships between entities within the network. It involves plotting entities as nodes and connections as edges between nodes. There are specialized variations of network analysis, including:

- route optimization

- social network analysis

- spread prediction, such as the spread of a contagious disease

The following is a simple example based on ice cream sales for the application of network analysis for route optimization.

Some ice cream store managers are complaining about the time it takes for delivery trucks to drive between the central warehouse and stores in remote areas. On hotter days, ice cream delivered from the central warehouse to the remote stores melts and cannot be sold. Network analysis is used to find the shortest routes between the central warehouse and the remote stores in order to minimize the durations of deliveries.

Consider the social network graph in Figure 8.18 for a simple example of social network analysis:

- John has many friends, whereas Alice only has one friend.

- The results of a social network analysis reveal that Alice will most likely befriend John and Katie, since they have a common friend named Oliver.

Figure 8.18

An example of a social network graph.

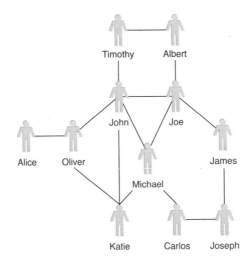

Sample questions may include:

- *How can I identify influencers within a large group of users?*

- *Are two individuals related to each other via a long chain of ancestry?*

- *How can I identify interaction patterns among a very large number of protein-to-protein interactions?*

Spatial Data Mapping

Spatial or geospatial data is commonly used to identify the geographic location of individual entities that can then be mapped. Spatial data analysis is focused on analyzing location-based data in order to find different geographic relationships and patterns between entities.

Spatial data is manipulated through a Geographic Information System (GIS) that plots spatial data on a map generally using its longitude and latitude coordinates. The GIS provides tooling that enables interactive exploration of the spatial data, for example measuring the distance between two points, or defining a region around a point as a circle with a defined distance-based radius. With the ever-increasing availability of location-based data, such as sensor and social media data, spatial data can be analyzed to gain location insights.

For example, as part of a corporate expansion, more ice cream stores are planned to open. There is a requirement that no two stores can be within a distance of 5 kilometers of each other to prevent the stores from competing with each other. Spatial data is used to plot existing store locations and to then identify optimal locations for new stores at least 5 kilometers away from existing stores.

Applications of spatial data analysis include operations and logistic optimization, environmental sciences and infrastructure planning. Data used as input for spatial data analysis can either contain exact locations, such as longitude and latitude, or the information required to calculate locations, such as zip codes or IP addresses.

Furthermore, spatial data analysis can be used to determine the number of entities that fall within a certain radius of another entity. For example, a supermarket is using spatial analysis for targeted marketing, as shown in Figure 8.19. Locations are extracted from the users' social media messages, and personalized offers are delivered in realtime based on the proximity of the user to the store.

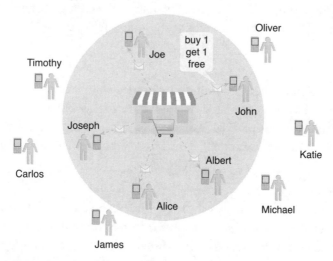

Figure 8.19
Spatial data analysis can be used for targeted marketing.

Sample questions can include:

- *How many houses will be affected due to a road widening project?*

- *How far do customers have to commute in order to get to a supermarket?*

- *Where are the high and low concentrations of a particular mineral based on readings taken from a number of sample locations within an area?*

CASE STUDY EXAMPLE

ETI currently employs both quantitative and qualitative analyses. The actuaries perform quantitative analysis through the application of various statistical techniques, such as probability, mean, standard deviation and distributions for risk assessment. On the other hand, qualitative analysis is performed during the underwriting stage, where a single application is screened in detail to get an idea of risk level—low, medium or high. Then, the claim assessment stage analyzes a submitted claim to get an inclination as to whether or not that claim is fraudulent. Currently, ETI's analysts do not perform any intense data mining. Instead, most of their efforts are geared toward performing BI using data from the EDW.

The IT team and the analysts applied a range of analysis techniques in pursuit of finding fraudulent transactions during the data analysis stage as part of the Big Data analytics lifecycle. Some of the applied techniques are presented here.

Correlation

It is noted that a number of fraudulent insurance claims occur right after a policy is bought. To verify this, correlation is applied to the *age of policy* and the *number of fraudulent claims*. A result of -0.80 shows that a relationship exists between the two variables: the number of fraudulent claims decreases as the policy gets older.

Regression

Based on this discovery, the analysts want to find out how many fraudulent claims are submitted based on the *age of policy*, as this information will help them to determine the chance that a submitted claim is fraudulent or not. Consequently, the regression technique is applied by keeping the *age of policy* as the independent variable and the *number of fraudulent claims* as the dependent variable.

Time Series Plot

The analysts want to find out whether or not the fraudulent claims are time-dependent. They are particularly interested in finding out if there are any particular time periods in which the number of fraudulent claims increases. A time series of fraudulent claims for the past five years is generated based on the number of fraudulent claims that were calculated each week. A visual analysis of the time series plot reveals a seasonal trend that shows that the number of fraudulent claims goes up just before a holiday and toward the end of summer. These results suggest that either customers make false claims in order to have money for the holiday period or they upgrade their electronics and other goods after a holiday by reporting damage or theft. A few short-term irregular variations are also found, which, upon closer inspection, are discovered to be linked with catastrophes like floods and storms. The long-term trend suggests that the number of fraudulent claims is likely to increase in the future.

Clustering

Although all of the fraudulent claims are different, the analysts are interested in finding out if any similarities exist between fraudulent claims. A clustering technique is applied that groups different fraudulent claims based on a number of attributes, such as customer age, policy age, gender, number of previous claims and frequency of claim.

Classification

During the *utilization of analysis results* stage, the classification analysis technique is used to develop a model that can differentiate between a legitimate claim and a fraudulent claim. For this, the model is first trained using a dataset of historic claims, in which each claim is labeled as either *legitimate* or *fraudulent*. Once trained, the model is brought online, where newly-submitted, unlabeled claims are classified as fraudulent or legitimate.

Appendix A

Case Study Conclusion

ETI has successfully developed the "fraudulent claim detection" solution, which has provided the IT team experience and confidence in the realm of Big Data storage and analysis. More importantly, they see that they have achieved only a part of one of the key objectives established by the senior management. Still left are projects that are intended to: improve risk assessment for applications for new policies, perform catastrophe management to decrease the number of claims related to a calamity, decrease customer churn by providing more efficient claims settlement and personalized policies and, finally, achieve full regulatory compliance.

Knowing that "success breeds success," the corporate innovation manager, working from a prioritized backlog of projects, informs the IT team that they will next tackle current efficiency problems that have resulted in slow claims processing. While the IT team was busy learning enough Big Data to implement a solution for fraud detection, the innovation manager had deployed a team of business analysts to document and analyze the claims processing business process. These process models will be used to drive an automation activity that will be implemented with a BPMS. The innovation manager selected this as the next target because they want to generate maximal value from the model for fraud detection. This will be achieved when it is being called from within the process automation framework. This will allow the further collection of training data that can drive incremental refinement of the supervised machine learning algorithm that drives the classification of claims as either legitimate or fraudulent.

Another advantage of implementing process automation is the standardization of work itself. If claims examiners are all forced to follow the same claims processing procedures, variation in customer service should decline, and this should help ETI's customers achieve a greater level of confidence that their claims are being processed correctly. Although this is an indirect benefit, it is one that recognizes the fact that it is through the execution of ETI's business processes that customers will perceive the value of their relationship with ETI. Although the BPMS itself is not a Big Data initiative, it will generate an enormous amount of data related to things like end-to-end process time, dwell time of individual activities and the throughput of individual employees that process claims. This data can be collected and mined for interesting relationships, especially when combined with customer data. It would be valuable to know whether or not customer defection rates are correlated with claims processing times for defecting customers. If they are, a regression model could be developed to predict which customers are at risk for defection, and they can be proactively contacted by customer care personnel.

ETI is seeing improvement in its daily operations through the creation of a virtuous cycle of management action followed by the measurement and analysis of organizational response. The executive team is finding it useful to view the organization not as a machine but as an organism. This perspective has allowed a paradigm shift that encourages not only deeper analytics of internal data but also a realization of the need to incorporate external data. ETI used to have to embarrassingly admit that they were primarily running their business on descriptive analytics from OLTP systems. Now, broader perspectives on analytics and business intelligence are enabling more efficient use of their EDW and OLAP capabilities. In fact, ETI's ability to examine its customer base across the Marine, Aviation and Property lines of business has allowed the organization to identify that there are many customers that have separate policies for boats, planes and high-end luxury properties. This insight alone has opened up new marketing strategies and customer upselling opportunities.

Furthermore, the future of ETI is looking brighter as the company embraces data-driven decision-making. Now that its business has experienced benefit from diagnostic and predictive analytics, the organization is considering ways to use prescriptive analytics to achieve risk-avoidance goals. ETI's ability to incrementally adopt Big Data and use it as a means of bettering the alignment between business and IT has brought unbelievable benefits. ETI's executive team has agreed that Big Data is a big deal, and they expect that their shareholders will feel the same way as ETI returns to profitability.

About the Authors

Thomas Erl

Thomas Erl is a top-selling IT author, founder of Arcitura Education and series editor of the *Prentice Hall Service Technology Series from Thomas Erl*. With more than 200,000 copies in print worldwide, his books have become international bestsellers and have been formally endorsed by senior members of major IT organizations, such as IBM, Microsoft, Oracle, Intel, Accenture, IEEE, HL7, MITRE, SAP, CISCO, HP and many others. As CEO of Arcitura Education Inc., Thomas has led the development of curricula for the internationally recognized Big Data Science Certified Professional (BDSCP), Cloud Certified Professional (CCP) and SOA Certified Professional (SOACP) accreditation programs, which have established a series of formal, vendor-neutral industry certifications obtained by thousands of IT professionals around the world. Thomas has toured more than 20 countries as a speaker and instructor. More than 100 articles and interviews by Thomas have been published in numerous publications, including *The Wall Street Journal* and *CIO Magazine*.

Wajid Khattak

Wajid Khattak is a Big Data researcher and trainer at Arcitura Education Inc. His areas of interest include Big Data engineering and architecture, data science, machine learning, analytics and SOA. He has extensive .NET software development experience in the domains of business intelligence reporting solutions and GIS.

Wajid completed his MSc in Software Engineering and Security with distinction from Birmingham City University in 2008. Prior to that, in 2003, he earned his BSc (Hons) degree in Software Engineering from Birmingham City University with first-class recognition. He holds MCAD & MCTS (Microsoft), SOA Architect, Big Data Scientist, Big Data Engineer and Big Data Consultant (Arcitura) certifications.

Paul Buhler

Dr. Paul Buhler is a seasoned professional who has worked in commercial, government and academic environments. He is a respected researcher, practitioner and educator of service-oriented computing concepts, technologies and implementation methodologies. His work in XaaS naturally extends to cloud, Big Data and IoE areas. Dr. Buhler's more recent work has been focused on closing the gap between business strategy and process execution by leveraging responsive design principles and goal-based execution.

As Chief Scientist at Modus21, Dr. Buhler is responsible for aligning corporate strategy with emerging trends in business architecture and process execution frameworks. He also holds an Affiliate Professorship at the College of Charleston, where he teaches both graduate and undergraduate computer science courses. Dr. Buhler earned his Ph.D. in Computer Engineering at the University of South Carolina. He also holds an MS degree in Computer Science from Johns Hopkins University and a BS in Computer Science from The Citadel.

Index

ABOUT THE SERIES

The Prentice Hall Service Technology Series from Thomas Erl aims to provide the IT industry with a consistent level of unbiased, practical, and comprehensive guidance and instruction in the areas of IT science and service technology application and innovation. Each title in this book series is authored in relation to other titles so as to establish a library of complementary knowledge. Although the series covers a broad spectrum of service technology-related topics, each title is authored in compliance with common language, vocabulary, and illustration conventions so as to enable readers to continually explore cross-topic research and education.

servicetechbooks.com/community

ABOUT THE SERIES EDITOR

Thomas Erl is a best-selling IT author, the series editor of the Prentice Hall Service Technology Series from Thomas Erl, and the editor of the Service Technology Magazine. As CEO of Arcitura Education Inc., Thomas has led the development of curricula for the internationally recognized Big Data Science Certified Professional (BDSCP), Cloud Certified Professional (CCP), and SOA Certified Professional (SOACP) accreditation programs, which have established a series of formal, vendor-neutral industry certifications. Thomas has toured over 20 countries as a speaker and instructor. Over 100 articles and interviews by Thomas have been published in numerous publications, including the Wall Street Journal and CIO Magazine.

**Cloud Computing:
Concepts, Technology
& Architecture**
by T. Erl, Z. Mahmood,
R. Puttini

ISBN: 9780133387520
Hardcover, 528 pages

**SOA with Java: Realizing
Service-Orientation with
Java Technologies**
by T. Erl, S. Roy, P. Thomas,
A. Tost

ISBN: 9780133859034
Hardcover, 592 pages

**SOA with REST: Principles,
Patterns & Constraints for
Building Enterprise Solutions
with REST**
by R. Balasubramanian,
B. Carlyle, T. Erl, C. Pautasso

ISBN: 0137012519
Hardcover, 577 pages

**Cloud Computing
Design Patterns**
by T. Erl, R. Cope,
A. Naserpour

ISBN: 9780133858563
Hardcover, 528 pages

**Big Data Fundamentals:
Concepts, Drivers
& Techniques**
by P. Buhler, T. Erl, W. Khattak

ISBN: 9780134291079
Paperback, ~ 250 pages

SOA Design Patterns
by T. Erl

ISBN: 0136135161
Hardcover, 865 pages

**Web Service Contract
Design & Versioning for SOA**
by T. Erl, A. Karmarkar,
P. Walmsley, H. Haas,
U. Yalcinalp, C. Liu,
D. Orchard, A. Tost, J. Pasley

ISBN: 013613517X
Hardcover, 826 pages

**SOA Governance:
Governing Shared Services
On-Premise & in the Cloud**
by S. Bennett, T. Erl, C. Gee,
R. Laird, A. Manes,
R. Schneider, L. Shuster,
A. Tost, C. Venable

ISBN: 0138156751
Hardcover, 675 pages

**SOA with .NET & Windows
Azure: Realizing Service-
Orientation with the
Microsoft Platform**
by D. Chou, J. deVadoss,
T. Erl, N. Gandhi,
H. Kommalapati, B. Loesgen,
C. Schittko, H. Wilhelmsen,
M. Williams

ISBN: 0131582313
Hardcover, 893 pages

**Next Generation SOA:
A Concise Introduction
to Service Technology &
Service-Orientation**
by T. Erl, C. Gee, J. Kress,
B. Maier, H. Normann, P. Raj,
L. Shuster, B. Trops,
C. Utschig-Utschig, P. Wik,
T. Winterberg

ISBN: 9780133859041
Paperback, 208 pages

**Service-Oriented Architecture:
A Field Guide to Integrating
XML and Web Services**
by T. Erl

ISBN: 0131428985
Paperback, 534 pages

**Service-Oriented
Architecture: Concepts,
Technology & Design**
by T. Erl

ISBN: 0131858580
Hardcover, 760 pages

**SOA Principles of
Service Design**
by T. Erl

ISBN: 0132344823
Hardcover, 573 pages

SOA & Cloud Computing Training & Certification

SOA Certified Professional (SOACP)

Content from this book and other series titles has been incorporated into the SOA Certified Professional (SOACP) program, an industry-recognized, vendor-neutral SOA certification curriculum developed by author Thomas Erl in cooperation with industry experts and academic communities and provided by SOASchool.com and training partners.

The SOA Certified Professional curriculum is comprised of a collection of 23 courses and labs that can be taken with or without formal testing and certification. Training can be delivered anywhere in the world by Certified Trainers. A comprehensive self-study program is available for remote, self-paced study, and exams can be taken world-wide via testing centers.

Dozens of public workshops are scheduled every quarter around the world by regional training partners.

All courses are reviewed and revised on a regular basis to stay in alignment with industry developments.

For more information, visit: **www.soaschool.com**

www.soaworkshops.com • **www.soaselfstudy.com**

Cloud Certified Professional (CCP)

The Certified Cloud Professional (CCP) program, provided by CloudSchool.com, establishes a series of vendor-neutral industry certifications dedicated to areas of specialization in the field of cloud computing. Also founded by author Thomas Erl, this program allows IT professionals to learn and become accredited in common and specialized topic areas within the field of cloud computing.

The Cloud Certified Professional curriculum is comprised of 21 courses and labs, each of which has a corresponding exam. Private and public training workshops can be provided throughout the world by certified Trainers. Self-study kits are further available for remote, self-paced study in support of instructor led workshops.

All courses are reviewed and revised on a regular basis to stay in alignment with industry developments.

For more information, visit: **www.cloudschool.com**

www.cloudworkshops.com • **www.cloudselfstudy.com**

PEARSON VUE

All Arcitura exams are available at Pearson VUE testing centers and via Pearson VUE Online Proctoring